Klaus Schaack
Why do German Companies
Invest in Apprenticeships?

For Lukas

Klaus Schaack

Why Do German Companies Invest in Apprenticeships?

The "Dual System" Revisited

KLAUS SCHWARZ VERLAG · BERLIN

Bibliografische Information der Deutschen Bibliothek:
Die Deutsche Bibliothek verzeichnet diese Publikation
in der Deutschen Nationalbibliografie;
detaillierte bibliografische Daten sind
im Internet abrufbar unter: *http://dnb.ddb.de*

© 2008 Klaus Schwarz Verlag Berlin

1st edition
Layout: textintegration.de
Cover illustration: © Carmen Steiner, fotolia.com

Printed in Germany

ISBN: 978-3-87997-348-4

www.klaus-schwarz-verlag.com

Content

Foreword

Within UNESCO, the UNESCO-UNEVOC International Centre for Technical and Vocational Education and Training (TVET) serves as a laboratory of knowledge and information on TVET with a particular reference to innovative and best practices in education for the world of work.

To facilitate exchange of this information and knowledge, UNESCO-UNEVOC is in the process of developing an extensive publications programme. The purpose of this programme is to acquaint education decision-makers and policy-makers with innovations, best practices and cutting-edge developments in TVET, to help develop and renew education systems in Member States to achieve greater quality, equity and relevance in their TVET programmes.

In compliance with its methods and purposes, UNESCO-UNEVOC has supported the preparation of this essay. The essay is an attempt to understand the German apprenticeship system, known as 'the dual system of vocational education and training', as a phenomenon embedded in a particular political, economic, cultural and educational environment.

One of the main issues explored in the essay is the investment behaviour of German companies with regard to financing training programmes. Despite a widespread perception among international TVET experts that companies usually do not invest in entry-level vocational training, German companies have been admired for their often lavish funding of training. The 'dual system' became a blueprint for many international efforts, mostly governmental in nature, designed to emulate the German training system. Unfortunately, due attention was not always paid to the conditions behind the success of the dual system. Both inside and outside Germany, there have been difficulties in understanding why German companies' investment behaviour deviates so sharply from international patterns of financing training programmes.

To understand the reasons why German companies invest in apprenticeships, this essay explores salient features of German apprenticeships in order to analyze how they interact with their political, cultural, social, educational and economic environment. The essay also examines the purpose-oriented design and planning of the German concept of 'Apprenticeship', a system which in Germany has been successful by tradition, with the result that its tertiary education sector is much smaller than comparable sectors in other economically advanced countries.

While the transfer of 'dual system' from Germany to other countries has been rarely successful, one basic feature of the system is still attractive to many policy-makers and training experts around the world – that is, the linkage between training (or TVET) institutions and the companies and/or the labour market, in addition to the concomitant practice-oriented nature of training.

In order to identify the main features of the complexity of the German 'Apprenticeship' concept, the author reviews several important traits of the German political system and the German political economy. He also examines the German education and training system, which gradually emerged during the foundation years of Germany's economic dynamism in the second half of the 19th century, as well as after World Wars I and II.

The author asserts that philosophical and biological concepts and theories of society are still enshrined in structures which came into existence in former times, and which still show a remarkable capacity to persist even under conditions of a so-called 'knowledge-based economy and society'. The text presented here contributes to the literature on 'Varieties of Capitalism' (in addition to 'Varieties of Democracy') from the angle of training, supporting the concept that different balances between political and economic values in different societies have effects on political, and education and training systems.

The author further argues that the notion of a 'Dual System', which underlies the German concept of apprenticeship, refers not only to the interplay of company-based training that is enhanced by vocational school education, but also to the intricate relationship between the companies' political and economic interests.

The chapter on financing of training is particularly interesting because it attempts to explain the 'miracle' of financing in an unorthodox way. While this is true for many countries, Germany's political and social landscape offers special opportunities to the private sector to shape the younger generation – a fact which does not appear to be fully understood internationally. The author argues that companies have wider interests than just profit-making, and explores how these interests find expression in companies' and private sector education and training policies. German companies take on apprentices not so much for economic, social responsibility or for image improvement reasons, but rather do so because of the privilege of designing and implementing mass-relevant training standards, and shaping the skills, competences, attitudes and mentalities of the younger generation. This feature is particularly relevant to the role of apprentice training in German politics and economy.

The final chapter speculates about the future of Germany's economic development. It takes fundamental educational reform as one of the prerequisites for a return to a fully-fledged economic dynamism and as one of the conditions required to successfully combat unemployment.

The author emphasizes that the German model of vocational apprenticeship is a particular but, nevertheless, exemplary model of vocational apprenticeship, because its concept is considered to be useful for handing down technical competences in a number of labour market niches as well as on a mass scale to the labour market in general. At the same time, he highlights the importance of the tertiary education sector as a necessary means to future German economic performance in a period of increasingly knowledge-based processes.

This publication can be employed as a reference for explaining the virtues and flaws of the German educational system in general, and its repercussions on German economy and society. It also teaches that training should be understood in the context of its wider environment, rather than merely through analyzing or comparing isolated training models.

This essay will be useful to individuals and institutions engaged in TVET who wish to gain information on the German model of apprenticeship, including its history and politics and especially with regard to the purpose of the German approach to apprenticeship.

A short version of this essay will also be published in the UNESCO-UNEVOC International Handbook of Education for the Changing World of Work which will appear at the end of 2008.

On behalf of UNESCO-UNEVOC, I wish to acknowledge the tremendous expertise and commitment of the author, Mr Klaus Schaack, and thank him for his efforts in bringing this essay to a fruitful completion. My special appreciation goes to the Klaus Schwarz publishers (Berlin, Germany) for the support they have provided to this publication project.

Rupert Maclean
Director
UNESCO-UNEVOC International Centre
for Technical and Vocational Education and Training
Bonn, Germany
18 June 2008

Acknowledgments

Every author owes thanks to the people who have supported him in one way or another. I am deeply indebted to the late Prof. David Wilson (University of Toronto/Canada), who had the kindness to polish my English and who made a couple of proposals in order to improve the clarity of my text. In the same vein, I would like to express my gratitude to Prof. Dieter Timmermann, rector of the University of Bielefeld/Germany, who offered valuable critical advice and comments on the essay presented here. During the last two decades, I had several opportunities to cooperate with Prof. Jon Lauglo (University of Oslo/Norway). Pleasant and fruitful conversations with him have left their traces in my paper. Last but not least, I am thankful to Dr. Rupert Maclean, Director of the UNESCO-UNEVOC International Centre for Technical and Vocational Education and Training, who made this publication possible.

Of course, the author is entirely responsible for the remaining weaknesses and mistakes of the essay.

Klaus Schaack

Introduction

The past is not dead. It's not even the past.
William Faulkner

Mass apprenticeship "systems" offer training on very different levels of quality for a number of economic sectors. Training quality may vary between very distant extremes and offer bright future perspectives for some, but not for others. Apprenticeships and the employment of helpers can include various forms of systematic, intentional and not so systematic, non-intentional and informal learning, imitation, copying, creative improvisations, solid work and botched jobs; but also personal dependencies of various kinds. Sweatshops using apprenticeships as a disguise for oppressive and exploitative forms of cheap labour still exist and forced child labour too. Hence, international apprenticeships deserve a second look for what they really are. But, apprenticeships exist in much gentler forms too and can be useful for handing down technical competences to younger generations either in a number of labour market niches only or on a mass scale on the labour market in general. Some countries traditionally manage to do that successfully: Austria, Germany, Switzerland and Denmark. Norway seems to have joined this group of countries more recently. But, good apprenticeships' records are not confined to economically advanced European countries. Also in Africa, Asia and Latin America apprenticeships can play a valuable training role, although their scales may vary considerably (see: K.-F. Schaedler, 1983; D. Bas, 1988; D. Bas, 1989; M. W. Coy (ed.), 1989; Ministry of Foreign Affairs/Danida, 1994, p. 45; J. Singleton (ed.), 1998; BIT (ed.): C. Maldonado et al., 2001). The following text deals with Germany only.

The entry-level age for apprenticeships in economically advanced countries has risen by several years after World War II. Throughout the first half of the 20th century and during the fifties, German children, for example, became apprentices usually in the age of fourteen (see for example: E. Hylla, 1928, S. 4/5), while the average entry-level age at present has come close to twenty. In the German case apprenticeships are complemented by vocational schools and other training provisions, offering a rather limited measure and spectrum of "theory" to apprentices of differently "capable" companies, but quality remains a reason why the training system can be christened a chameleon, though not the only one (see, for instance: M. Leidner, 2001). Examining the notions, which are used to describe the German vocational education and training system, a striking variety of terms can be found: apprenticeship system, a training system for "handarbeitende Fachkräfte" (manually working specialists) (G. Kerschensteiner, J. A. Wissing et al.), a "system of two authorities" (E. Spranger, H. Wander), "dualist system" (J. Zabeck), "vocational training and school system" (H. Abel), dual system, cooperative system, a system of company-based vocational training complemented by school-based education, vocational education system, (initial) vocational training system, vocational education and training system. Other expressions to be found are: corporatist, neo-corporatist or "traditional-corporatist" (W.-D. Greinert) training system, governmentally controlled market system or governmentally accompanied market system. If we would include the notion "Berufslehre" in our list (used in the German-speaking regions of Switzerland) another aspect would become visible: apprenticeships aiming for a *Beruf* (vocation, calling). Still the question remains, which of the features of the "dual system" can be regarded as the "constitutional elements" (see: D. Konietzka, 1999, S. 53 – 63).

The diversity of terms is no accident, as the "dual system" is a multi-faceted arrangement. It underwent a couple of innovation processes during a period of more than 100 years because of technological and organizational reasons and skinning because of different political aspirations, needs and conditions. After World War II it was subject to strategic policies first to preserve it and to re-establish the pre-Nazi framework, later to transfer an arrangement under the dominance of the private sector to some sort of public responsibility or even to change its character more fundamentally (see: M. Baethge, H. Solga, M. Wieck, 2007, S. 19). Such policies were linked to the Federal Vocational Training Act (BBiG) from 1969 and further reform proposals of the Brandt government in the early seventies, which failed. Concerning the Act from 1969, the German Chambers have published the following statement: "The Act made no alteration in the training system itself" (DIHK (Hrsg.) 2003, p. 14), a view which is confirmed by non-partisan statements: "In essence the basic structure was not changed by the Vocational Training Act from 1969" (F.-X. Kaufmann 2003, S.

301; a condensed overview of the historical development of the "dual system" is offered by D. Konietzka, 1999, S. 45 – 53)

The "theory" often applied to the combination of apprenticeships plus vocational school lessons can be summarized as follows: *manual* work = practice in companies + *brain* work = trade-related theory in vocational schools! The introduction of the term "dual system" in 1964 implied an "educationalization" of the arrangement "in theory" without changing facts, based on the so-called concept of the "learning places". "Theory" took the company as a learning place, which it can be in its own way, besides being an economic undertaking. In 1987, roughly twenty years after the Vocational Training Act became effective, rather fundamental innovations occurred concerning the design of training standards, *not mirrored* in the unchanged label "dual system", when the new industrial training ordinances for metal-working and electrical vocations were introduced. They can be regarded as the starting point of novel and innovative developments concerning the addition of "generic", "core" or "key competences" to technical competences and concerning the upgrading of training standards from mainly "manual" to mainly "knowledge-based" – in a couple of areas, but not in all of them.

Recent "model experiments" (pilot projects) try to overcome the often "dualistic" organization of training processes between companies and vocational schools (highly instructive empirical findings about "cooperation", including a typology of companies' "cooperation activities" with vocational schools are offered by Berger, K./G. Walden 1995), sometimes by the establishment of a bureaucratic mechanism called "cooperation office", sometimes by new approaches to curriculum design and didactical concepts (for the former: H. Bau/Th. Stahl (Hrsg.) 2002; for the latter: M. Reinhold 2002, S. 44 – 48). Whatever they may achieve or not achieve, the "model experiments" as such stress the fact that the German arrangement of companies and vocational schools still is not capable to guarantee a homogeneous and well-integrated training process everywhere and in all training vocations (see also: W. R. Heinz, 1994, S. 112; D. Euler, 1998, S. 118 – 130). After a period of more than hundred years which have passed since the "dual" arrangement of companies and vocational schools began to emerge, a rather remarkable outcome, which offers food for thought!

Because of its multifaceted and permanently changing character (though differently in different branches and areas) and because of the ideological character of many theories about the "dual system", it is still a phenomenon difficult to describe. It includes many divergent aspects, but not necessarily the same everywhere and in all trades. Nevertheless, a proposal, how its basic features can be understood, will be offered in box 2. For Th. Deißinger the term "dual system" is an artifact: the "wrong label on the wrong item" (Deißinger 2001, S. 15). In his opinion the term hides the "particular functional processes and their determining factors" (S. 16), hence the logic of the "system". This is, what the paper attempts to illuminate.

The conceptualization of "training models" can be helpful for international training comparisons. They have a capacity to support the understanding, how general education and TVET "systems" are organized in this or that country and which differences exist internationally. But, some reservations are necessary. It is especially necessary, that the "bones" of the model are covered by "some flesh"; analyses and explanations how and why the model functions and how and why it is structured in this or that way. Theoretical models turn into problems, when neatly isolated constructs based on generalities "produce" international transferability assumptions. Often contexts remain either amorphous or unexplained, which frequently means the same. In life, such constructs are often peculiarly interwoven with other facts and conditions: political circumstances, economic needs, cultural legacies, particular state-society-configurations as unplanned results of history, the roles of private sectors, the tasks of chambers and economic sector organizations, the educational efforts of populations and the size and shape of their demand for different kinds of education and training. They all differ internationally, not just to a certain degree, but sometimes widely and in a number of dimensions. Like individually and oddly shaped elements of a *multi-dimensional* puzzle, they are linked to each other in a "systemic" way: elements fit into one specific place in a certain "puzzle", but not into any other space in any other "puzzle". They defy copying therefore. "It appears impossible, to exchange individual subsystems for "modules" which are alien to the system, because the overall system is closely linked in its individual components, it derives a large part of its success from that fact" (W. Abelshauser 2003, S. 188; *my translation – K. Sch.*).

An understanding of the German economy like this can be called "systemic". "Systemic linkages" of "systemic modules" in the framework of a bigger whole generate an evolutionary path-dependence as they cause specific transformation patterns of national economies in case of internal or external pressures; a clearly different understanding of the term "systemic" compared to the meaning of the term in Luhmann's theory.

It is one of the purposes of this paper to offer a sketch of the "strange puzzle" of which the "dual system" is a part. A closer look may reveal that the "puzzle" might be less "strange" than it had looked at first sight. It shows "annual rings" – so to speak – similar to trees; historical events from different economic and political periods have left their traces. What may look strange in the beginning, peculiar institutional arrangements for instance, are basically clues for our understanding. The reasons for German companies' "participation" in training vary between economic/financial, marketing, recruitment, but include political reasons too.

This paper deals mainly with the *political* reasons. The chapter on "Financing Training in Germany – Companies' Reasons" will also touch other reasons for the financing of apprenticeships. A detailed analysis of economic reasons would be desirable as they play an important role in apprenticeships – though a different one in differently sized companies. But, it is difficult to get hold of sufficiently disaggregated empirical data, if they exist at all: normally private sector training "systems" are less transparent than public ones.

The paper therefore concentrates on the linkage between training and the dominant private sector influence in the design and implementation of training standards. Training design under the dominant influence of their own "private interest government" without major interference by other social groups or factors is in fact vital for the companies' training motivation. But, it is important to understand that small companies, especially in the crafts sector, can have a differently shaped training motivation because of short-term *economic* (profit-making) reasons. In the past such companies were an essential component of the stability of the "dual system", as they had a "sponge function" in periods of crises: they recruited apprentices when bigger companies didn't do that in sufficient numbers. But, the "sponge function" of smaller companies seems to be a phenomenon of the past.

The bigger companies' goal bundles in training include a variety of micro-economic policy goals in recruitment, public relations, HRD and image policies, but also wider political interests which are the focus of this paper. Political private sector interests are often sidelined in the scientific literature on "costs and financing of training", particularly when the German political context is not sufficiently taken into consideration. Assumptions about the obligations of private companies to observe "profitability" in a narrow sense easily become spurious, when such assumptions construct a contradiction between economic goals and a wide range of other goals in the service of the economic ones. Companies certainly don't through their money "out of the window" but carefully weigh what they have to pay and what they get or what they are able to maintain by investment in training, namely a rare privilege in parliamentary democracies!

Companies (like individuals) operate in structures and some structures offer incentives to companies to invest in training while other structures don't and this is basically a very pertinent reason, which makes a difference. It is not sufficient therefore to simply compare advantages (benefits) and disadvantages (costs) of apprenticeships with school-based training modes. The comparison has to include a much wider circle of issues. Certain training modes may have their (temporary) economic advantages, but may include disadvantages in other areas, maybe even more important ones. But, such topics and questions are subject to normative evaluations, which yield different outcomes in different situations and countries, because of their particular political histories and circumstances.

A sufficient level of incentives in parliamentary democracies for entrepreneurs' "participation" in the production of "vocational skills and competences" is a rare phenomenon, not because of political neglect, but because of the usually prevailing marginal conditions in such democracies: not everything can be combined with everything successfully. Arrangement "alpha" includes a certain combination and level of intended and unintended effects including opportunity costs, and arrangement "beta" another combination. Choice becomes a choice between alternatives which both offer different opportunities and different drawbacks. Policy-makers have to decide which are preferable or less detrimental and hopefully these decisions are in line with popular aspirations and democratic principles of some weight.

Parliamentary democracies in industrially advanced countries, which cannot offer a sufficient level of incentives for the production of "vocational skills and competences" to entrepreneurs (on the secondary level or in non-formal modes) tend to develop functionally equivalent institutional solutions. They are usually to be found in a more diversified field of tertiary education, hence, not on the assumed "home grounds" of TVET. Societies opting for such a development path, instead of the more traditional combination of general and vocational mass education on the secondary level plus training in the non-formal mode, might have hit the path to economic success in the period of "knowledge-based economies and societies" by sending large percentages of their young population to diversified tertiary institutions. "Tertiary education for all!" seems to be the slogan of recent times (see: OECD (ed.), 1989), especially in East Asia, and other countries are free to learn from East-Asian success (or not).

The paper pulls together different aspects of German society, not least from the educational underpinnings of the "dual system" and from the German governmental concept. It is rather lengthy which is justified by the fact that the question, why German entrepreneurs invest in training is both intriguing and not easy to understand, if one deems "culturalist" explanations not fully satisfying. Five boxes illustrate terms, backgrounds and definitions relevant for the understanding of the German training system, four of them taken from the relevant literature.

German training is often identified with the "dual system", although the "dual system" is only a part of what occurs in the training sector. In fact, German training takes place in different modes of delivery:

- the "dual system"
- the full-time vocational school system
- the so-called "transition" system
- training provisions within tertiary education.

While the "dual system" for a long time was the politically and numerically dominant "system" within the traditional modes of delivery, it lost its numerical dominance during the last decade. "Dual" training decreased from 51% to 43% of the new training entrants, while the so-called "transition" system reached the level of 40% and the full-time vocational school system 17%. The problem of this structure is mainly concentrated in the "transition system", because it includes around half a million of young people in training programs with little vocational perspectives and high labour market risks. (see: M. Baethge, H. Solga, M. Wieck, 2007, S, 7)

Box 1: Apprentice and Apprenticeship

** The apprentice is "a servant, who is chained to work over a couple of years in favour of a master craftsman under the condition that the master craftsman teaches him in this trade." (Adam Smith, Eine Untersuchung über Natur und Wesen des Volkswohlstandes, 1. Buch, Jena 1920, S. 157) – (original title: The Wealth of Nations: An Inquiry into the Nature and Causes [1778])*
** "The one is an apprentice, who, obliged to work, undergoes a regular training over several years in a company in order to learn a certain occupation." (Anton Graff, Der Lehrling in der Industriearbeit, M. Gladbach 1925, S. 13)*
** Apprenticeship is "in the majority of all cases the company-based training of youthful candidates of a vocation which regularly takes place because of an apprenticeship contract between the master craftsman and the apprentice." (Eugen Schindler, Artikel "Lehrlingswesen" im "Handwörterbuch der Staatswissenschaften, 4. Auflage, 6. Band)*
** "Apprenticeship is essentially a combination of education and industry. It is a process of learning by doing, under which a minor is taught the art of a trade by one who is at the moment engaged in it; the minor paying either in whole or in part for this instruction by the work done on objects destined for the master's consumption or sale."*

The first three quotations were taken from: H. Rosenberg, Die Berufsvorbereitung des Industriearbeiters und ihre Bedeutung im Kampf um die Arbeitsfreude, Koeln 1930, S. 14 und 15; my translations – K. Sch.; the fourth quotation was taken from: Paul Howard Douglas, American Apprenticeship and Industrial Education, New York, Columbia University, 1921, p. 217.

Box 2: How to Understand the "Dual System"?

The German "dual system" consists of an apprenticeship core (supported by training in group training centres) and a part-time vocational school appendage. Like other apprenticeship "systems", the German apprenticeship "system" is mainly based on companies' training capacities. A major particularity of modern German apprenticeships is to be seen in the application of the company-overarching, janus-faced Beruf *concept, defined in the bargaining processes between private sector and trade union representatives. It can be understood as a bundle of competences and a particular mass mode of socialization, social integration and stratification, unlike that prevailing in other western countries.*

Thus, training is (mainly) company-based, *but includes complex aims, tasks and processes, which cannot be described as being simply* company-oriented, *though it is the case to a considerable extent. The essential duality, hence, consists of the market mechanism and private sector plus trade union self-regulation, according to the* Beruf *concept, valid nation-wide. The company – school duality is asymmetric and often more dualistic than dual, but rather fictitious as a description of the "system's" basic mechanism because the roles of the vocational school are not fundamental, but rather are complementary.*

The Beruf *offers a curriculum frame which moulds German training and is in the same time a labour market regulator – not imposed, but accepted as a bargaining result between the "social partners" – and elevated to legal status by governmental seal. Each training* Beruf *(different from* Beruf *as an occupation) defines those bundles of vocational competencies regarded as essential in various fields of gainful employment for* berufliche Handlungskompetenz *(vocational action competence).*

The didactic dominance of practice *in companies is important for the generation of a highly particular type of competence, which has been historically effective in shielding skilled workers' social space against differently qualified intruders, but also limiting skilled workers' range of opportunities, thus generating strong borderlines between various social groups.*

The "dual system" is a legally invigorated and fine-tuned, self-administered mass apprenticeship arrangement of the private sector with some trade union influence, supported by different government levels by different means. The "dual system's" integration into public responsibility and into the overall German education "system" is peculiar and precarious because private sector ownership and management of the apprenticeship core was not uplifted, but confirmed by the Vocational Training Act from 1969. Ownership, "philosophy", design and supervisory mechanisms and "educational" contents and aims do not fit smoothly into a public education "system" controlled by parliaments and ministries, operating (or functioning) as the trustees of voters' decisions, because general education and vocational training follow different principles and aims.

Apprenticeships are dependent upon the economic cycle, like in other countries, despite countervailing legislation. Apprenticeship standards are subject to formal, but non-substantial, ministerial supervision. The "dual system" is a particular training track officially situated on the upper secondary level and prepared and fed by the differentiated education "system", but not exclusively from the different lower secondary tracks. It is a separate, but not a stand-alone, phenomenon in a larger "system of communicating components". The "dual system" is one of the main reasons why the German higher education sector is much smaller than comparable sectors in other economically advanced countries.

The German Government Concept after World War II

Post-War Deliberations and Some Consequences
in Education and Training

The atrocities and the war crimes of the 'Third Reich' caused a search for institutional arrangements in its aftermath, designed to prevent their repetition. Allied powers and German politicians ascribed them essentially and with good reason to the 'absolute power' of the Nazi state. Making the re-emergence of 'absolute power' in German politics unlikely was a complex task, not easily achieved, as politicians were doubtful about the German population. Therefore, the politicians drawing up the "Basic Law" became "constitutional fathers without constitutional people".

In democracies people are regarded as "the source of government's authority and (under various substantial restrictions) even of its politics" (B. Williams, 2002, p. 210). To perceive the people as politically unreliable necessarily imposes considerable obstacles on the drafting of a constitution and requires precautionary measures to be taken. This is what happened in the German post-war situation. Theodor Heuss, the first president of the Federal Republic of Germany, for example, warned about the people as if he would speak about a vicious dog (see: H. H. v. Arnim, 1993, S. 23). Foreign observers had similar misgivings (see: K. v. Beyme, 1999, S. 69).

Attitudes like these bestowed a deficit on the German provisional constitution: politicians did not dare to make the electorate directly involved in selecting the deputies for the "Parliamentary Council", drafting the "Basic Law", which were chosen from among the deputies of the different "Länder" parliaments. It is, therefore, not astonishing, that the German "Basic Law" was conceived as a "pure" representative provisional constitution (K. Sontheimer/W. Bleek, 200, S. 29). The voting system also avoided the voters to exert a "direct" influence by *not* adopting an English-style "first behind the post" arrangement but (predominantly) a "representative" system, which favours electoral lists on which candidates rank according to pure party decision. But, there is a difference between the two, which might be of some interest. The English model seems to be more capable to generate some "trust" between the voters and the elected deputy of a constituency including a moral indebtedness of the elected representative vis-à-vis his/her election base. The German electoral lists produce a fairly fair picture of the relative strength of the electoral will, but the relation between the constituency and the elected representative seems to be much slacker. 'People's sovereignty', as a democracies underpinning principle, was recognized, but in a way, which widely dispersed the electorate's influence and rendered it as indirect as possible. In addition, democratic principles were combined with other principles like 'self-administration' or 'social (group) partnership' and, perhaps even more important, influential legal experts understood "democracy" as "party democracy" (see: W. Hennis, 1973, S. 135 – 143; * W. Hennis 1998, S. 107 – 135; W. Hennis 1998, S. 136 – 141; S. Benoehr 1999).

Because of such reasons political parties, indispensable in a parliamentary democracy, and other organizations might have got more

---

* Hennis' analysis includes highly pertinent remarks on the social background of parliamentary deputies and on educational promotion practices: "That a civil servant cannot be in the same time a member of parliament is self-understanding for Englishmen or Americans. We Germans, in the contrary, have become used to the fact that the majority of all deputies in regional and in federal parliaments are members of the civil service. That a competent educationist can support his promotion in order to become a school director, if he is an owner of a party membership card, I cannot deem more worthy than being qualified as a reserve officer or by students fencing bouts." (W. Hennis 1973, S. 143; *my own translation* – K. Sch.) "Reserve officer" and "students fencing bouts" were – among other things – taken as indicators of a person's position in the social "pecking order", and of closeness to "values" appreciated during the "Wilhelminian Empire", not least of a dashing mentality (kurzangebundener Schneid, "Mumm in den Knochen"): all too often nothing else than an expression of snobbishness (Standesdünkel), but in contemporary promotion policies it could be understood – and all too often was – as more important than a person's educational, managerial or other qualifications and experiences (see also: Chr. von Krockow 1999, S. 130 – 135, on the same topic, on "berufliche Pflichterfüllung" and on the particular Prussian blend of Lutheranism and Calvinism). It goes without saying that the numerical dominance of "civil servants" ("Beamte" and "Angestellte") over deputies from other social backgrounds in the present German parliament fits well into the described political frame and can also be seen as a result of precautionary stabilization policies favouring more "security"-oriented elements of German society, not so much liberal, entrepreneurial or free-wheeling spirits: certainly a difference to Anglo-Saxon approaches. While the separation of powers is generally strong in Germany, such practices, on the other hand, undermine the democratic principle to separate legislative and executive powers.

than their due share in the democratic process and seem to have become rather "independent" from citizens.

The principle of 'people's sovereignty' does not apply to the German training sector, or, at least, only in a watered-down version, despite the fact that, for many years after World War II, a large number of German youngsters was "educated" in apprenticeships – a fact of undeniable social and political relevance, so far beyond parliaments' and ministries' power to determine the curricula (training standards). The training sector's importance for the German economy radiates into the general education "system" as well and strongly influences the size of sub-sectors, structures, curriculum contents including the opportunities to "climb" from primary to various forms of lower secondary, to various forms of upper secondary and, finally, perhaps, to various forms of tertiary education. Contrary to many other educational "systems", especially one-track "systems", which can be compared to an "elevator", the German three-track system can be more adequately compared with a "sorting machine", which unfortunately but intentionally includes a kind of social sorting. Still, the basic structure of the German educational system can be described as a three-track system, but, while it is also possible to describe it as a four- or five-track system, some states of the German federation (Länder) seem to be on their way to a double track system. The question is, if such developments are mainly caused by educational or political deliberations, or by demographic developments (see for instance: E. Rösner, 2007).

The Structure of German Government

Though politicians of the Allied Powers and German politicians did not develop congruent concepts and differed in a number of fields (for instance in education and training), there was a wide acceptance in "both camps" that the future political structures of Germany should be non-centralized, federal and democratic. Therefore a small number of older German "Länder" (states) re-emerged, like Bavaria and, later, Saxony, while most of them were newly created (like Baden-Wuerttemberg, Rheinland-Pfalz or, later, Mecklenburg-Vorpommern). Besides features of a strong federalism exercising power in education, cultural affairs, radio, television, law enforcement, the organization of the bureaucracy and the regulation of local communities, another characteristic feature of the German political "landscape" is the strong separation of legislative, executive and jurisdictional powers, stronger than in many other countries.

The *decentralization of governmental powers* in different dimensions (separation of powers, federal structure) is complemented by a *centralized society*, centralized by organizations of social groups, some of which are not only very influential, but taking part in public affairs in a number of circumscribed fields, not least various organizations of the employers like BDI (Federal Association of German Industries), BDA (Federal Association of the German Employers) and the German Chambers of Industry and Commerce, the German Chambers of the Crafts and others, organizations which were successors of those organizations which originally were endowed with certain legal rights in the end of the 19th or in the first half of the 20th century. But not only the employers formed strong associations, employees and workers did as well, as can be seen from the trade unions and their umbrella organization, the DGB (Deutscher Gewerkschaftsbund = Federation of German Trade Unions). A popular German textbook for students of political sciences holds the opinion: "Compared with the organized system of power of the corporations (Verbände) the political weight of the parties seems to be secondary." (K. Sontheimer/W. Bleek 2002 (14. edition), p. 198).

Though the government can be deemed superior to all the other actors in the political arena, in German *interlocking politics* government has to accept *two sources of political sovereignty*: its own, of course, based on the voters ballots, but also the political legitimacy of the "social partners". The cooperation pattern of intermediate organizations, acting as "private interest government" and government proper, consisting of patterns of collusion and conflict, constitutes a major part of German *interlocking politics* in which government and the peaks of employers' organizations and trade unions and the self-administering bodies of the private sector (chambers) are integrated in a neo-corporatist arrangement, which widens and strengthens the power base of government on the one hand and in the same time weakens and circumscribes democratic government as an independent political player. It goes without saying, that there are repercussions on the influence of the electorate, which is diminished. The role of the "social partners" as a second source of political legitimacy is not considered fully democratic.

In particular fields *neo-corporatist arrangements* add something to the power of elected government. State administration is mediated by self-government in a couple of sectors and the official rationale for such a policy design is the hope that governmental intervention might respond more to social needs and be technically more informed. The organizational solution found in the design of quasi-public organizations can take the form of a "clearing house", which is assumed to have a functional advantage. Such designs should "act like political shock-absorbers. ... They tend to limit political controversies ... And they limit the scope of policy initiatives." (P. Katzenstein 1987, p. 58).

They *blur the distinction between state and society* by causing intimate interaction between the peaks of social groups and government and they have a not so democratic side effect: they hold "a broader political constituency at bay" (P. Katzenstein, 1987, p. 32). There is a built-in tension between such mechanisms producing "public" decisions and parliaments, and it could be argued, that neo-corporatist arrangements devalue the role of parliaments in the formulation of legitimate norms in a democratic state. Some schools of political thought observe such quasi-public institutions and norms formulated by neo-corporatist arrangements, despite their assumed functional efficiency, with suspicion or misgivings.

Despite being a precautionary political concept of the post-world-war-II-situation, the policy of a *wide dispersion of power* can also be traced back to German traditions: Germany consisted for a long time of an array of regional units (kingdoms, duchies, counties etc.), while a kind of power sharing was institutionalized in cities between the city government and the guilds. By sharing its power with the representation of social group interests the city government became weaker and stronger in the same time, already in medieval times. It forged alliances with them, but also had to give in to some of their demands, thus avoiding centrifugal forces becoming effective. In some fields, not least in training, this traditional "division of labour" can be regarded as a part of the German "collective memory", relevant for the rejuvenated designs after World War II, when the "absolute power" of the Nazi state was dismantled.

The consequence of the design based on four major structural phenomena, namely federation (1), separation of governmental powers between legislation, execution and jurisdiction (2), a circumscribed inclusion of social groups in governmental tasks in a couple of particular fields (3), quasi-public institutions (4)) is not a complete rupture of the power of German federal governments, but its taming.

It seems to be typical for German politics that major reforms can only be pushed through when the bigger parties, the Christian-Democratic Union (CDU) together with their organizationally independent Bavarian relatives from the Christian-Social Union (CSU) and the Social-Democratic Party of Germany (SPD) manage to design a compromise. This, in all likelihood, also has to include that (major) parts of the reform are agreed upon not only by the "Bundestag", but also by the "Bundesrat", the second chamber representing the 16 German states.

It is unlikely that the representatives of the chambers, major business interests or the trade unions are sidelined in the process, which does not mean, that they can push through their own intentions, in a robust way, but a complete and rude rejection of their proposals could cause major political revulsions in the German political system, which therefore is often called a "consensus system".

Sometimes the two chamber system cannot produce a decision, or only when the "Vermittlungsausschuss" (mediation committee) becomes involved. Bargaining takes place in the "chambre separee" and often governmental and opposition parties claim victory, while all the positive aspects are ascribed to the own and all negative aspects to the other position. Usually a large number of citizens is puzzled what really has taken place and which organization is responsible for which parts of the new law; a process which is not helpful for citizens' political education.

Taken all the different features and designs together, the taming effect is produced which the "founding fathers" of the Federal Republic had in mind, fearing misguided voters and the absolute power of a central government in the hands of despotic persons. The tamed power of German federal government is the reason, why the American political scientist P. Katzenstein has called his analysis of the German political system (before unification): "Policy and Politics in West-Germany – The growth of a Semi-sovereign State" (Philadelphia, 1987). German politics, including federal government and the German Chancellor, has to observe the rules of *interlocking politics*. Major reforms and changes need the assent of many sides (government, partly the opposition too via the "Bundesrat" and top organizations of "civil society" including the trade unions) and this is the strength, and in the same time, the weakness of present German politics. The strength is continuity; the slow grinding of sharper policy tools, or only a compromise, gradual change, incremental progress and the forging of a solution (decision) supported by many.

The weakness is the difficulty or even the impossibility of achieving fast and fundamental reform, when such reforms are needed, or even a blockade of decision-making. In recent years critical observers might get the impression that the decision-making processes between federal and regional governments and parliaments have gotten rather intransparent, not rarely producing skewed and sub-optimal results. Only when the situation is really pressing the two bigger parties and maybe the "Verbände" can be forced into obedience to the need, that further "politicking" (partisan politics in order to blame the opponent or to marginalize him/her as a contender) is not what is needed any more, but to look for a "reasonable" solution satisfying the citizenry and the needs of the country. Unfortunately, there is neither an automatism nor a guarantee that this will occur!

The "Governmental" Role of Private Sector Organizations (including the Trade Unions)

The four major structural phenomena described above are the causes of the close circumscription of the German federal government's power. German government has to obey more numerous and more severe constraints than most other governments. The "division of labour" between government proper, "private interest government" by the "Verbände" and chambers and the processes going on in 'para-public' institutions are an obstacle for the comprehension of German politics by visitors from foreign countries, which do not implement such designs in their own "political landscape" and might reject them not without reasons.

The role of the "Verbände" and chambers vacillates and shimmers and can be seen in different illuminations: on the one hand, they can act as pressure groups, pressurizing the government. On the other hand private sector organizations have a tendency to "attack" the trade unions, while the trade unions "attack" the employers' associations. But sometimes, associations thought to be natural opponents are able to join forces. In addition, while colluding with the government, their leaderships must remain in contact with their members, for instance, the employers' associations cannot be sure that, what they have agreed upon with government, finds the support of various types of enterprises and the same is true for trade unions and their members. Mediation of different interests requires sensitivity and the mediators themselves easily can "fall between two stools". Last, but not least, they (employers' associations and trade unions) can act as "public entities", designing "public regulations", rubber-stamped by government into law if they are capable to find a common position, e.g. in the case of training ordinances (standards).

The "Verbände" have – as far as training standards are concerned – a capacity to act *de facto* "in lieu" of government, like government or, as government by aggregating their views after the completion of bargaining processes and then channelling them via "clearing houses" into the legal bulletin (Bundesgesetzblatt). The government merely rubber-stamps the results of the bargain and is needed as an official notary. The eminence of the role of private sector organizations in German political life, sometimes even in public roles, is no accident, but a remnant of corporatist concepts.

Germany cannot trace back its foundation as a nation-state to a strong democratic tradition, though democratic movements and elements were *not absent* in her history. But, unlike England, which transformed herself gradually over a longer period of time into a democratic nation by various major steps and reforms, unlike France, which started its modern development after "theoretical preparation" in a major violent upheaval in 1789 under the guiding ideas of "equality, liberty and fraternity" and unlike the Swiss variation of the gradual development of a localist-populist (communal) democracy (Wilhelm Tell can be taken as a paragon of a populist hero fighting an outside intruder into the local community), Germany was unified in 1870/71 "from above", but not guided by a democratizing or humanizing idea of the new state (again, such concepts were not absent, but forced to stay in the wings).

The unification of 1871 took place under the aristocratic leadership of a rapidly rising and rapidly industrializing nation, taking her pride from economic and industrial progress and pre-democratic Prussian values. Emphasizing her military, organizational, administrative, economic and other skills, Hugo Preuß, principal author of the "Weimar" constitution, complained about the lack of political skills and the "otherness, which separates our political structure from nearly all other modern civilized people." "Political passion lacks political understanding. This is not astonishing, where should it come from? It requires tradition and a long history." (H. Preuß, 1916, S. 164 and S. 170)

Be it as it may: no democratizing guiding principle at hand, or only weakly, Germany had to rely on older Prussian military, bureaucratic and newer industrial virtues, often viewed from other parts of Germany with mistrust, but, in the final consequence had to be accepted, although sometimes only grudgingly (see: H. Plessner, 1982, S. 53/54; Chr. v. Krockow, 1999, S. 47 – 66).

The keywords of German development, therefore, became "Leistung" (performance), with a strong connotation of economics ("wirtschaftliche Leistung"), and "social security", because of Bismarck's stick and carrot policy vis-à-vis the social-democratic workers' movement during the German ascent after 1871; an ideology, which was revitalized after World War II. Economic performance (see the popularity of the cigar-puffing Ludwig Erhard, the first Minister of Economic Affairs and later chancellor) and "social security" hold their pre-eminent place in German consciousness up to present times.

The wide dispersion of power in Germany, though it can be traced back to older traditions, is largely the result of precautionary policies, which included strong precautionary elements against an electorate, which yet had to prove her "democratic worth". It fit well into a framework intending to disperse power, when training remained under the supervision of the private sector despite the disliking and contradictory statements of American educational commissions and US-led military governments (see for instance: G. W. Ware, 1952; Kw. Stratmann/M. Schloesser, 1992, S. 54/55; B. Rosenzweig, 1998), which regarded the German education and training system as one of the stabilizing forces of Nazism and especially the training component less an educational than an economic sub-system.

The German state apparatus, because of such reasons, is less monolithic than in comparable cases. It is more like a conglomeration of departments and levels extended by the inclusion of social forces, drawn into the governance of circumscribed sectors, the training sector in particular. Partly because of the *partial* fusion of state and society by "pulling" associations (Verbände) into the realm of governmental tasks ample consultation processes have to take place before reforms can be implemented, not sweeping but incremental reforms. "…, responsibility for many key policy areas in the FRG lies outside the boundaries of the state altogether. 'Para-public' institutions' such as the Bundesbank and chambers of commerce are private bodies invested with public power, and are protected against central government by administrative and constitutional law (Katzenstein 1987)" (St. Wood, 2001, p. 254). The German state, thus, is less an actor, who imposes the will of the people on society filtered by parliament, but "a set of institutional relations linking the public and the private sector which impinges on politics." (P. Katzenstein, 1987, p. 372) This constitutes a rather interesting difference to Japan, the other nation which had her governmental system reframed after World War II by external designs: " …, the collective effect of government in Japan is toward a national cohesion and centralization rather than toward the dispersion of power and the institutionalization of conflict. The Japanese state is capable of making decisions and of enforcing them once made." (T. J. Pempel, 1982, p.16)

Box 3: The Historical Roles of the Guilds

"The analysis of the functions of guilds shows a complex, multi-layered organization. Economic, political, social, religious and cultural aspects can be identified.

In principle two main functions can be recognized. One concern was the protection of a status-adequate income of the craftsmen by regulation, for instance by compulsory guild membership, the other one to gain influence in city politics or even to achieve a share of city power. Besides these main functions social activities played a role, e.s g. the support of the sick and the poor, welfare activities in ecclesiastical affairs, last honours in funerals and the support of cohesive emotions through symbols and garment rules."

Because of the two main functions of the guilds researchers tend to explain their roles either by the economic interests of their members, the craftsmen, or by the sovereign role of guilds in the regulation of economic life in European cities.

"Two aspects shall be remembered in the end of this chapter:

First: the urban associations of the middle ages, founded because of economic, social and religious purposes, were without exception vocation-related.

Second: The guilds were share-holders of a public city culture. They were responsible for the training of the young generation in crafts skills and commercial affairs. The members of the guilds had to become used early in life to rules and methods of a vocational socialization (…)."

(Extracts from E. Schoenfeldt, Berufsbezug, zentrales Merkmal der deutschen Berufsausbildung, Kassel 2002, S. 51/52/53; my translation – K. Sch.)

"Basic" Training Models and the Particularity
of German Apprenticeships

Historical Development and "Basic" Models

Recent theorizing about international training "systems" has not always been consistent. While some authors insist that training "systems" are the result of different national histories including the international influences on them, others try to design "basic models" of such training "systems" and end up with the construction of two basic models: a market model (*dispersed competition,* but also *spontaneous coordination*), and a governmental model (*hierarchical control; control by law)* or a school-based and a company-based mode of delivery of technical and vocational education and training (TVET). These basic models can also be described as: coordination by the market forces (see: box 5) versus coordination by (legal) coercion. The basic models then allow the design of "mixed" or "dual" training models, which *combine* a "regulation circuit of the market" and a "regulation circuit dominated by laws and bureaucratic rules". Sometimes, both positions ("training "systems" are the outcomes of history" and the "basic models" view), are presented by the same author in the same text.

Such "model-platonistic" designs, as Hans Albert once criticized neoclassical economics (see: H. Albert 1998, S. 114 – 126; first published 1963), are still phenomena in recent reasoning about training. Once, the two models are identified as "basic", an "optimization operation" beyond space and time can take place: when the "regulation circuits" of the "state" and "the market" are combined, "mixed" or "dual systems" emerge and they leave history and circumstances behind.

Whatever the social, economic, political, cultural etc. conditions are, "dual" training can be defined as "optimal": linking theory and practice, being mass-relevant, inexpensive (*even if the contrary is true*), contributing to innovative dynamics, raising productivity and product quality, reducing youth unemployment, being "very modern" and other desirable outcomes. Major disadvantages do not seem to exist, if at all. By the conceptualization of the category "TVET system" or "training system" the world is perceived through pre-structuring glasses, as if everything would neatly fall into clear-cut categories. The phenomena to be investigated, consequently and inevitably, become varieties of "training systems".

But, it cannot be excluded before sufficient analyses have been carried out that some "training systems" are a peculiar mixture of different components and do not simply belong to the "training" category and nothing else. When, regardless of circumstances and in any case, blended areas or sectors and multi-functional "systems" are *a priori* excluded by the theoretical design, investigations might not grasp a number of historical, functional and structural features relevant for the understanding of the "training system" under scrutiny and its performance (perhaps even decisive ones).

This paper emphasizes the need to take history more seriously. "Basic models" should only be designed, when numerous international studies exist which do not simply put certain terminological "hats" on varying circumstances, but investigate existing varieties including those, which blend training with other "social sub-systems". Nowadays, such "hats" all too often are in the neoclassical fashion, which "de-socializes" training arrangements and takes their historical character away. But, the market "hat" and the governmental "hat" cannot be deemed an exhaustive description of the world's multi-faceted features and there are more processes, structures and institutional arrangements, than neoclassical theory accepts. Other institutions, in the consequence, are easily called "market limitations", "market imperfections", "imperfect markets", "market barriers" and the like in neoclassical theory or are treated as traditional phenomena, which, because of social inertia or unknown reasons still exist. The underlying implication often is that they will or have to disappear in the course of time, not least in an era of "globalization".

Different geographical and political circumstances, different foreign influences, different religious believes etc. have resulted in the different structural and institutional endowment of countries, hence, in different ways how they generate social order. "Institutions provide the basic structure by which human beings throughout history have created order and attempted to reduce uncertainty in exchange. ... They connect the paths with the present and the future so that history is a largely incremental story of institutional evolution ..." (D. C. North, 1990, p. 118)

When economics is not only taken as a science concerned with the production and sales of goods and services, bearish or bullish expectations, rates of return, flows of money, "payments generating payments" – in Luhmann's manner of speaking -, but as a historical science taking the different ways into consideration how economic activities are pursued and structured in different countries, differences can be identified how "productive capacities" are generated in different societies including the "processing" and "shaping" of human beings in education and training "systems". It should also be possible then to compare with some measure of precision which effects and consequences are concomitants of one or the other way: obviously an important matter as can be seen from ongoing international benchmarking efforts and from more serious comparative work investigating how societies function and how they can be modernized, reformed or partially changed.

History has brought forth a bewildering wide variety of technical and vocational education and training "systems" in different contexts and the differences still persist. The variety also consists in economically relevant quantitative differences, for which reasons have to be identified. These differences need to be analyzed first before fruitful theorizing about "types", "models" and "systems" can take place. The side-by-side existence of the "training systems as an outcome of history" hypothesis and the hypothesis of "two basic models" is an expression of the fact, that the needed international and comparative studies have not yet been sufficiently carried out. The "basic models" approach is often based on "pure economics" of the Walras type or neoclassical theory following the footsteps of Alfred Marshall, which do not sufficiently describe social contexts and structures and consequently do not offer a well-designed theory of social and institutional change. The most popular, recent textbooks of economics present the basic institutions of the modern world simply as a "market and state" dichotomy (Samuelson/Nordhaus 1998, 15. Auflage, S. 50 – 66; Samuelson/Nordhaus 17th edition, 2001, pp. 25 – 45). While deliberations about "imperfect competition", the "informal sector" or "ethnic problems" and other factors structuring labour markets are mentioned and analyzed, the treatment of such structures is far from exhaustive. Especially institutions alien to Anglo-Saxon circumstances and relevant for training and gainful employment in other countries are not presented.

Often "the state" (or "government") and "the market" are introduced in economics and vocational training research as self-understanding entities of the same or similar nature all over the world. Differences between markets and states in different countries are insufficiently taken into account and are usually understood as "homogeneous" and – concerning employers and employees – "the only nexus is cash" (C. Kerr 1954, p. 95).

But, meanwhile, many specialized studies have given evidence that neither working places in different companies and branches are the same, nor their endowment with more or less sophisticated machinery. Some work places are attractive, some are "difficult-dirty-dangerous" ("three-d"), some are high paying, some are in sweatshops, some are intellectually, others physically demanding, others require long and specialized preparatory manual training, which can be offered by some workers, but not by others, while other workplaces can already be occupied by workers after one or two training days only etc. Workers in general need and have different qualifications and competences. But, nearly inevitably, other institutions intervening into labour market and training affairs unknown to the Anglo-Saxon world – as mentioned above – are usually conspicuously absent in international TVET analyses. The inclusion of such institutions is essential for the understanding of the "dual system". "Other institutions" besides "markets" and "governments" at least *prima facie* need to be taken as facts of life, not as desirable, undesirable, or more or less desirable.

In some countries it is rather obvious that "the nexus" between employers and employees is not only cash, but other facts as well, for instance, a particular "Beruf" in Germany, which requires a training period of three years or more. Such workers are not likely to join the "everybody" segment of the labour market except in emergencies or in cases of clearly higher wages in the "everybody" segment which is unlikely.

Or, in Korea, a tendency of workers at least in larger enterprises to keep a certain "loyalty" to an employer beyond the "cash nexus" and a complementing tendency to insist on the employers' "loyalty" as well which perhaps can be traced back to a "familistic" understanding of the firm and which, be it as it may, makes hire and fire policies a very conflictive issue indeed. Simply quitting a job because of financial reasons might not be appreciated and also "firing" therefore often has produced in Korean circumstances extremely hard conflicts, including very physical encounters between workers and police.

"Markets" and "states" are generalities and markets can be markets of "perfect competition", they can be dominated by oligopolies or monopolies, they can be homogeneous, dualistic, or segmented into even more segments. Markets can be shaped *by other institutions* in various ways, and they can deal with different types of raw material, agricultural goods, industrial semi-products or products, symbols, labels, trade marks, advice, services of an extremely heterogeneous nature etc., for which market mechanisms differ considerably. Hence, "regulation by market laws" includes a wide variety of ways and means by which regulation occurs and how "the market" is shaped by human interaction – itself shaped by different "institutions" in different ways in different countries and cultures. The formula "regulation by market laws" begs many questions and does not explain much of the phenomenon to be scrutinized.

On labour markets people offer educational qualifications (usually certified by educational documents), labour market relevant competences (usually certified by training, testing and/or work documents) and such qualifications and competences are not the same across nations, neither are mentalities or values. They are based on different cultural and other underpinnings, follow different principles and inclinations and thus, are differently "cut".

Analogous reasoning applies to "regulation by legal stipulations and bureaucratic control". "States" can be centralized or de-centralized, they can be ethnically homogeneous or ethnically heterogeneous, there can be a dominating ethnic minority ruling the state, or a dominating ethnic majority, states may impose a "state religion" or "ideology" on her citizens or may be religiously or ideologically tolerant. "Legal stipulations and bureaucratic rules" can be promulgated by democratic as well as by despotic states. States may apply democratic rules comprehensively or may mix them with other principles and they may transfer certain rights to social groups or institutions (chambers for instance) and organizations representing such groups. The Swiss example gives evidence that democratic rules can be applied in a mixed way by combining elements of a parliamentary democracy with elements of a direct democracy. Thus, as in the case of "regulation by the market circuit", "regulation by legal stipulations and bureaucratic rules" is – to a large extent – a non-explanation.

"States" and "markets" are globally relevant institutions, but their functions and shapes do not seem to be identical internationally. Associations and corporations play a role in many societies, but their functions and roles can be very far apart and the same is true for chambers, for instance. While some chambers are "transmission belts" for governmental policies, they are the expression of the private sector especially of powerful companies in other cases and defend their positions, views and interests. In other cases, again, they become private interest government responsible for circumscribed tasks in particular fields in a well-defined division of labour between government and chambers.

Such functional, institutional and structural differences can be traced back to a variety of historical reasons among which cultural concepts or different "webs of meaning" hold an eminent position. Decisions about the institutional woodwork of a nation taken at historical turning points "freeze" the chosen constellation and make it more permanent than it otherwise could have been. The arrangements found in such moments often have shown an incredible capability to survive many changes and the German "Dual System" is a case in point.

It is evident, that institutional arrangements, which mirror social, political and ideological forces, "fixed" in different moments in time and under varying conditions and influences (national and international) necessarily are different. Such differences have not yet been wiped out by globalization and a prediction, if it ever will happen, would amount to claiming prophetical gifts. There are still "particularities", some of which might be essential for the identity of a nation and not only no obstacles to economic effectiveness, but parts of its backbone. Such self-spun or man-made concepts solidify in structures and institutions – as already mentioned – like markets, states, clans, vocations, associations, castes, chambers etc. and though the terms in use are often identical internationally, they differ in contents.

The neoclassical binary (state, market) consideration needs to be complemented by other institutions in international analyses, if results are not to become biased. The theoretical model of neoclassical economics seems to be simple enough to become bolstered by popular reasoning, which quite rightly assumes that vocational training basically can be offered either in companies or in vocational schools, usually excluding "marginal conditions" from the analysis.

But this kind of a "schematic categorization" (model-platonism) is of little help. It does not offer insights, why some modes of delivery are widespread in some countries and operate on high levels of quality and quantity, but not in others, even when the countries compared operate on similar economic levels. In Switzerland, where different parts of the same country are on similar levels, it is a conspicuous fact, that apprenticeships are popular in German-speaking parts, but less popular in French- and Italian-speaking parts. In order to scrutinize such phenomena, the whole network of influential conditions in a certain country has to be understood, at least in its main components. Apprenticeship systems exist in many industrially advanced countries, albeit nowadays often on a small-scale only, while they are mass systems in Austria, Germany, and Switzerland.

Apprenticeships exist in France, in the UK, and in the United States. But, except in the Germanic countries, the importance of apprenticeship training is marginal in most countries. In Germany apprenticeships in the "dual system" accounted for the training of 40 to 70% of young age cohorts in recent decades and the "dual system" has become – especially after the foundation of the BIBB – a sophisticated and complex training system covering the training needs of small, medium-sized and large enterprises in many though not in all sectors of the German economy.

How can such differences be explained? The usual explanations offered for the large size of the German apprenticeship sector compared to other economically advanced nations inevitably seem to be "culture", "tradition", "customs" or "habits". Sometimes "tripartism" (state – employers – employees) is emphasized. Both explanations are not wrong, but not really satisfying. "Culture" and "tradition" rarely have a potential to trump hard-boiled entrepreneurial "calculations" (and these "calculations" are not necessarily confined to cost-benefit calculations) under any circumstances, neither in Europe nor in East-Asia nor elsewhere.

In the end of the day, in the business world there must be identifiable benefits of whatever kind. Of course, benefits might occur in various "currencies" and do not always and necessarily assume an immediate "cash value" in terms of money. However, in any case, entrepreneurs must be in a position to clearly identify and appreciate some kind of benefit of value for the pursuit of their business interests, whatever it may be. In such cases they are usually willing to invest, if there is a credible perspective or promise that a relevant benefit of some kind will accrue. As far as "tripartism" is concerned, it is in use in a number of countries and results are not always convincing.

When "a general perception exists that employers don't invest in VET" (Ko Yoo Jin 2003, p. 166) it is required to find a realistic explanation, why German entrepreneurs deviate from established patterns of international entrepreneurs' training behaviour and follow the opposite strategy. This explanation has to be non-idealistic and should not only emphasize motives like "culture", "altruism" or "social responsibility", but offer a more realistic view. It should give evidence that German entrepreneurs' behaviour in their home contexts is as sober and hard-nosed as the behaviour of international entrepreneurs not investing in training in the contexts of their home countries. It is certainly not the result of faulty mathematics on the side of German employers.

Box 4: The Company

"Business firms are specialized organizations devoted to managing the process of production. Production is organized in firms because efficiency generally requires large-scale production, the raising of significant financial resources and careful management and monitoring of ongoing processes."

(Extract from Paul A. Samuelson/William D. Nordhaus, Economics, 17th edition, New York 2001, p. 119.)

Box 5: The Market

"The market system is a mammoth coordinator through mutual adjustment and is especially adapted to the difficulties of coordination in the face of scarcity. Many of us – even some economists – believe that the market system coordinates economic behaviour and only economic behaviour, as though there exists some identifiable area of behaviour called economic, which is the only behaviour that the market system can coordinate. That belief has to be abandoned. The fact is that the market system coordinates an enormous range of behaviour, just what variety we do not yet know. Again, think society, not economy.

Although even Cro-Magnons traded with each other, probably using shells as money, we have seen from prehistory to the Industrial Revolution of the eighteenth century that buying and selling were for most people only adjunct methods of social coordination. Notwithstanding the development of trade routes in the ancient world, custom and political authority carried the burden of social coordination. Only in the last three centuries has much of it shifted to the market system. For a market system to become a mammoth coordinator, slavery had to give way to wage labour, and static feudal ties of worker to land had to be replaced by market transactions in labour and property. And the guilds' social control in the cities had to recede to allow freer buying and selling."

(Extract from: Charles E. Lindblom, The Market System – What it is, how it works, and what to make of it, New Haven and London: Yale University Press 2001, p. 35)

In the German case, taking history seriously means to move beyond the neoclassical binary (government, market) consideration and to use a multifaceted approach. Understanding German apprenticeships in terms of "learning places" or "regulation circuits" regularly fails to understand their particular features and their particular embedded nature.

The following institutions can be regarded as relevant for the functioning and structuring of training in Germany: Companies (1), markets (2), state (or government) (3), "Verbände" with a public status and "self-administration" (4), apprenticeships (5), *Beruf* (6), and a specifically structured general education "system" (7), and their interactions shape the workings and the outcomes of the so-called "dual system". Compared to these cultural, political and economic institutions and their interrelations, the vocational school is secondary in importance and will, therefore, remain outside the frame of this analysis.

The seven basic terms are interwoven and the workings of the "dual system" depend on the peculiar way, in which the "modules" are hooked up to each other. *Markets* imply *companies*, which are the major training providers and a particular frame for what can be learned and trained. If markets are not fuelled by dynamic companies training capacities will be either small or be not advanced. But, dynamism has more roots than just vocational training, or, a particular training mode, for instance, the general educational attainment level of the population, her maintenance and accumulation of "social capital", her "moral fibre", the stability and ambitions of families, the social fairness of work conditions in companies and institutions and the fairness of promotion and remuneration practices, governmental policies, popular work attitudes (ascetic/hedonistic) and a certain balance of cooperation and competition (many diverse things have to come fruitfully together). Mono-causal explanations often smack of one-sided interpretations in favour of certain interests and, therefore, "once again, multiple causation must be emphasized." (M. Olson, 1982, p. 152)

Markets and companies imply competition, but in German normative evaluation of competition in the end of the 19th century (the formative years of German capitalism after the foundation of the German empire in 1871), competition was seen as an anarchic tendency moving towards monopolies. American concentration processes and trusts were perceived as negative phenomena. Hence, regulation was seen as favourable, but, not mainly by government but by the self-constraint of market participants: social or economic self-regulation. The German historical school of economic science therefore promoted the view that the collective benefit of cooperation is higher than the sum of individual benefits generated by competition (see: P. Windolf, 2002, S. 423/424). Chambers and other associations (private interest government) "cartelize" the companies' training interests and such "cartelization" phenomena are more widespread in the German political economy than in genuinely liberal economies of the Anglo-Saxon type, not only in training. This is the reason, why some authors see the *Verbände* as one of the most important particularities of the German *corporatist* or *neo-corporatist market model.*

The German *state* concept (an outcome of history) includes a certain division of labour, in which the government "delegates" circumscribed tasks to the private sector. The sharing of power between government and "private interest government" sits uneasily upon the principle of popular sovereignty on which parliamentary democracies are based and often is perceived critically by observers of other national and cultural backgrounds used to other normative evaluations. In the German case, government, not least in training, "delegates" certain rights to the *Verbände*, or, the *Verbände* have somehow taken the right because of a "normative vacuum" or a "normative lack of clarity". The most popular term which describes this division of labour in German apprenticeship discussions therefore is "self-administration".

But, even not taking its administrative frame into account, German *apprenticeships* are different – for instance – from English apprenticeships: "In the UK apprenticeship has been concerned with specific skills, sometimes involving a narrow range of tools and equipment. There is no tradition of cross-sector employment for apprentices who complete training. Apprenticeship is seen as equipping trainees for specific and well-defined tasks, and has never been regarded as a training *process* on which a named range of skilled adult employment can be based." (P. Haxby, 1987, p. 176) Besides the difference concerning the training *process* the German concept of the *Beruf* is usually wider than the English concept of an "occupation". The two different principles are differently "cut" and while the systematic design of the training *process* is important in Germany, in modular or competence-based "systems" the emphasis is on "outcomes", thus, on "certification", while the *process* is still of minor concern. The *process*, of course, is not only important, because "training" has to follow "a well-designed path" in the German concept, but includes a socialization dimension, very different from the socialization processes taking place in schools. Attempts to harmonize different concepts in the frame of the "European Union", undertaken by CEDEFOP, have not been successful, and, most probably, both dimensions – training and socialization – have been involved in the outcome of CEDEFOP's efforts.

A *Beruf*, valid nation-wide, requires a cooperation of companies under the umbrella of *Verbände* to be established and an integrated perception of companies' training needs bundled into a common view; a strong admixture of other viewpoints by governments or other "outsiders" would diminish the linkage between the outcome of design processes and the willingness of companies to implement the design and to "invest" in training. A *Beruf* cannot be produced as a nation-wide concept by a single company, except, when this company plays the role of a monopolist in the area of competence development in question (the only company offering related apprenticeships).

Last, but not least, apprenticeship tracks are peculiarly and precariously integrated in the German education and training configuration, but clearly segregated from the genuine education tracks, thus, integration and segregation both apply to them.

Without the insertion of social and cultural filters into the German general education "system" against the educational advancement of larger percentages of young age cohorts in lower secondary education (at age ten) the German education system could not "shovel" youngsters into apprenticeship streams in such quantities etc. Therefore, the embeddedness of the "dual system" needs to be scrutinized in more detail in subsequent parts of this paper. Before this can be done, an introduction of the essential training concept, the *Beruf*, and the particular role of the *Verbände* in training is needed. The paper follows the view that societies are locked into their institutions largely shaped by cultural selection and that they are not loose heaps of sand which can be shaped arbitrarily by applying various internationally acclaimed moulds.

Analyses confined to the German training system or analyses using the perspective of international comparative training research all too often bypass the particularities of the "dual system" because of the too strict observation of a narrow research perspective focusing strictly on training and training provisions. Such approaches can necessarily neither detect the particular embeddedness of German apprenticeships, nor the "boosters" attached to various parts of the German "social machinery", and therefore tend to ascribe miraculous qualities to the "dual system", while overlooking its drawbacks.

The Beruf (vocation or calling)

Vocation and Work

The fact, that *Beruf* is an essential term for the understanding of German society, history and culture can be easily realized. Merely superficial contacts with Germans suffice to identify the fact, that their family names, in many cases, are denominations indicating a *Beruf* and/or a social station: Bäcker or Becker (baker), Bauer (peasant), Fischer (fisherman), Jäger (hunter), Köhler (charcoal burner), Korbmacher (basket weaver), Kupferschmidt (copper smith), Leinweber, Leineweber or Leinenweber (linen weaver), Metzger or Fleischer (butcher), Müller or Möller (miller), Schäfer (shepherd), Schmied, Schmid, Schmidt or Schmitt (smith, blacksmith), Scholz, Schulz, Schulze, Schultze, Schulte, Scholtes, Schultes, Schultheiss (mayor), Schreiner or Tischler (cabinet maker), Schumacher, Schuhmacher or Schuster (shoemaker), Seidenspinner (silk spinner), Töpfer (potter), Wagner (coach builder), Wannenmacher (literally: tubmaker; in fact a kind of a basket weaver), Weber (weaver), Winzer (vintner), Zimmerer, Zimmermann, or Timmermann (the north German variety of "Zimmermann") (carpenter) and so on. Sometimes such names were latinized in order to make them sound and look more distinguished as in Molitor = Müller or Piscator = Fischer and similar cases.

Beruf is linked to "Arbeit" (work, labour) and, in the past, Protestants in particular were obliged to fulfill their work duties with precision and to be diligent. "Beruf" requires a preparation period to induce people into the secrets and "tricks" of the trade, into the required skills and competences of a fully fledged manual specialist. Since the end of the 18th century work (labour) or labour power (Arbeitskraft) was regarded in Europe and in the US as a value-generating force. Economists, natural scientists and engineers from Adam Smith to Karl Marx, from Hermann von Helmholtz to Frederick W. Taylor thought about labour, labour power, and human energy as the driving forces behind the productivity of labour and economic progress (see: A. Rabinbach, 1992, especially chapter 2). But, experiments and strategies how to raise the productivity of labour advanced in different directions in different nations, but everywhere gave rise to vocational and technical education and training in an internationally wide variety of arrangements.

One method of raising labour productivity consisted in "rationalizing" the work process. The most known names representing this line of development are probably Frederick W. Taylor and Henry Ford. Complex work processes became subject to work analysis and work synthesis and in the final consequence re-arranged in a new way, cutting work into small pieces and depriving it from conceptual and planning tasks. Both processes included "de-skilling" and had not so favourable consequences on worker's motivations as work became extremely monotonous, boring and fatiguing. Cutting work into small pieces (jobs) is in line with unrestrained or "free" market principles and the American immigration society of the 19th century with many unskilled immigrant workers.

The German labour and training market followed and follows other principles, and includes other "institutions" than Anglo-Saxon labour markets. These institutions produce "rigidities", but also much vaunted effects on skills and competences. Certainly, there are rigidities which should be abolished, but there are "rigidities" which are caused by the basic concept, the *Beruf*, which is the heart of German self-understanding and therefore not easily to be extinguished, if one wants to avoid major economic and social woes. In the context of this paper, it is important to emphasize that *Beruf* shapes work in Germany, and therefore work on the labour market is not something undefined and divisible as one maybe would like it, but in entities called *Berufe*. On the labour market *Beruf* as a regulating principle in effect "produces" a large number of employment vocations or occupations. They have to be prepared in a much smaller number of training vocations for which training standards have to be defined and therefore *Beruf* also includes a curriculum and a didactical dimension.

The Beruf (vocation or calling): basic features

The concept of the *Beruf* is still the "principle" underlying German training and the distribution of labour market opportunities to individual persons. *Beruf* normally indicates a well-reputed middle-level position in the hierarchy of labour-market and social positions, while academic *Berufe* are called "Professionen" (professions). The concept of the *Beruf* (not "the dual system") is the essential principle of German training according to Th. Deißinger (1998) (actually he used the term "the organizing principle") and E. Schoenfeldt offered a rather similar view more recently (2002), calling "the reference to vocation", "the central aspect of German vocational education and training". A. Green (with A. Sakamoto) holds that "a long history of societal respect for technical skills and knowledge and for professional autonomy, encoded in the uniquely German concept of the *Beruf* (profession/occupation), has been comprehensively institutionalized in the Dual System of occupational training which prepares two-thirds of German youth for working life and serves to transform the majority of paid jobs into skilled occupations." (A. Green, 2001, pp. 62/63) In the following sub-sections this "uniqueness" of *Beruf* shall be explored in more detail.

Beruf originally had religious-ethical underpinnings. Its meaning can be traced back to a "vocation" or "calling" by God into a certain position and role in life, which should not be deserted. Nowadays *Beruf* is void of religious meanings, but not completely void of ethical dimensions. It is a multifaceted phenomenon: an exchange pattern of a certain area/level of competence and wages/salaries, the core of personal identity, a double-edged element of social stability/rigidity, a particular mode of socialization, a mechanism of social integration and stratification, a concept for the identification of social roles and positions, a bundle of specialized competences, a basis for an occupation of some duration and as such opposed to mere "jobs" and a labour market regulator (compare: W. Dostal, F. Stooss, L. Troll 1998, S. S. 438 – 460).

Beruf as a labour market regulator actually functions as a self-regulation principle of the private sector. It turns the German labour and training market from a "free market" in a "self-regulated market". The self-regulatory function of the *Beruf* has to be emphasized here, as the most popular *Beruf* definitions do not mention it.

While before 1500 the term *Beruf* has not been generally accepted and in many cases the term "Stand" (station) has been preferred, after Luther's translation of the bible (1522; the New Testament) the term started its *very slow ascent* to general use. Between 1500 and 1900 both terms coexisted and were used for the description of the same or similar social phenomena, while *Beruf* is dominant nowadays. In some parts of Germany, for instance in Prussia, the term "Stand" was used till 1929, or even longer. Sometimes *Beruf* and "Stand" merged into the term "Berufsstand" (vocational station).

According to Luther the "distribution of vocations" expressed God's will and for traditional society it was "natural" thus. A vocation should be a vocation for a lifetime: all vocations "were equal before God": "God does not care for the work activities, but for obedience. … That is the reason, why a pious maid, so she follows her orders and takes care of her duties and sweeps the courtyard or carries the manure to the field or a servant in the same vein takes care of ploughing or moving his cart, directly will go to heaven on the right road, while another one, who goes to St. James or to church, but does not care for his vocation (Amt) and work, directly will go to hell." (quoted from Chr. Mayer, 1999, p. 36)

The "equality of vocations before God" awarded dignity to the "common man". "It was what he had been waiting to hear, a recognition of his value as what he was". "This was a profound revolution in thought; it overturned not just medieval values, but those of classical antiquity and the renaissance too. Some were even prepared to place manual work above leisured mandarin pursuits." (A. Black, 2003, p. 111) Vocations may have been "equal before God", especially in reformation times and the equalizing perspective of the Lord must have given a boost to the crafts guilds, their members and their attempts to influence city government. But, times did not remain unchanged and in more religious than mundane matters vocations may have been "equal", while human evaluation usually arrived at different verdicts. Worldly wisdom usually placed different vocations on different rungs in the social hierarchy.

During the 19th century, *Beruf* became more popular, without replacing "Stand" completely. Especially after the foundation of the German Empire under Prussian dominance in 1871, the term *Beruf* was increasingly utilized, while *Stand* did not disappear. *Stand* emphasizes social inequalities and differences, which might have become politically undesirable, while *Beruf* expresses the same concept less offensively. The introduction of the occupational census (Berufszählung) in 1882 already used combined notions like "Berufsabteilung" and "Berufsart" (in the sense of economic branch), while the family members and servants were grouped according to the *Beruf* of the "family head". Only in 1925 the gainfully employed persons were grouped according to their own *Beruf* in the occupational census.

It is not surprising that *Beruf*, as a multifaceted phenomenon, has provoked a large number of definitions (see: W. Dostal, F. Stooss, L. Troll, 1998, S. 442). The most widely used definition is still Max Weber's (1864 – 1920) or variations or derivations of his definition: Beruf can be understood as "that specification, specialization and combination of performances of an individual, which for him/her are the basis of a continuous chance to earn a living." (M. Weber 1920, republished 1980, S. 80)

This definition is often abbreviated by an expression emphasizing that *Beruf* is a "bundle of competences". Though the abbreviation was chosen for good reasons, it should not be overlooked that *Beruf* is also a mode of socialization, social integration and stratification. Recent definitions therefore attempt to combine the aspects of competences, qualifications and performances of individuals with the overall performance of society. R. Raddatz several years ago has proposed the following definition:

"The vocation (*Beruf*) is, whatever the qualification level may be, the execution of activities lasting for a certain duration, which is paid and which consumes to a major part the work capacity and the working time. The vocation gives life its character and contributes to self-realization and personal development. The execution of a vocation (*Beruf*) secures the livelihood of the individual and creates the preconditions for the fulfilling of other tasks in society. It is economically meaningful and contributes to the overall performance of the society. In article No 12, the Basic Law of the Federal Republic of Germany guarantees everybody the right for a free choice of a *Beruf* as well as its free execution." (R. Raddatz, 1999, S. 50)

Important features of the *Beruf* can't be recognized by either of the two definitions. It is always emphasized in connection with German vocational training, that it is "practice-oriented", which is of a particular kind and not self-understanding. "Practice-orientation" *in gen-*

eral can be differently defined and, thus, include or exclude different matters like civic affairs including citizens' duties and liberties, economic and technological matters from agriculture to production-oriented services, playing musical instruments, technical/artistic drawing and sketching or physical and religious exercises. "Practice-orientation" can be focused on one area or cover a number of areas.

In the German case, because of the underlying concept of the *Beruf*, there is a very clear focus of "the dual system" on technical and commercial matters, while training in other areas is much smaller in numbers (e.g. in the liberal professions) or differently organized (e.g. in Berufsfachschulen). The relevant areas are sub-divided in competence claims and sheltered by vested rights. This was the traditional concept of the crafts and the guilds jealously guarded the areas which gave their members a chance to eke out a livelihood against any intrusion either by another guild or by people, who – in the eyes of the guild – didn't hold the "right kind" of qualification because they had not undergone apprenticeship with a member of the guild. Such people were regarded as botchers, bunglers or moonlighters even when they knew how to do the job and were competent to do it. The concept is still valid in a number of areas in the crafts, but has a capacity to disturb cooperation in industrial processes, when competence claims are vigorously defended, however the overall work task might be structured. Such competence claims are hardened by tariff contracts in which certain competence bundles and levels are the fundaments for payments.

The *Beruf* concept of the crafts was adopted by industries initially in 1926 in metal working industries, shipbuilding and chemical industries but reshaped for the industrial conditions, though examinations remained with the Chambers of the Crafts till the end of the thirties. The German industrial *Beruf* concept basically was a merger between the traditional concept of the *Beruf* and "taylorism" and thus the "de-skilling" tendencies of pure "taylorism" were not as dominant as in many other industrialized countries, though strong. By the generalization of the *Beruf* concept through its adoption in industries a new type of worker, the "Industriefacharbeiter" (skilled industrial worker) came into existence – a new social type, so to say. After the *Beruf* concept was extended from the crafts to industries it was finally stabilized and generalized in German society: at the end of the thirties of the last century. The cultivation of *Berufe* has consequences and implications for the education and training configuration.

Beruf in the crafts was associated with a satisfying life including a satisfying working life, while "taylorism" threatened to "empty" the *Beruf* concept in industries and, thus, threatened *Arbeitsfreude* (joy of work). H. Rosenberg's booklet from 1930 *"Die Berufsvorbereitung des Industriearbeiters und ihre Bedeutung im Kampf um die Arbeitsfreude"* (The vocational preparation of the industrial worker and its importance in the struggle for the joy of work) can be taken as a typical example expressing German misgivings or even "Angst" about the future in a "soulless" period of "mechanization" and "industrialization". Rosenberg's analysis started with the hypothesis that contemporary industrial workers have "no real intrinsic relation to their *Beruf* and that therefore life goes on without being a harmonious whole" (or: "without a harmonious unity"). The problem was not seen in the "social system" as such (whether capitalist or socialist), but as a consequence of "industrialization" and the "mechanization of companies" (see: H. Rosenberg, 1930, S. 109).

In order to make a big leap to recent times: In industrial areas, the *Beruf* concept has become modernized since 1987 and the design of the different industrial occupations and, hence, the training vocations too, became overlapping to some extent, thus enabling and promoting cooperation between differently competent people. An additional lubrication was introduced by the emphasis on "key competences". But, certain rigidities may have remained, though the approach has been softened and "enriched". The "cultivation" of modern skilled workers in industries and the crafts is still based on different educational tracks and a particular training and socialization process and does not enable them to proceed to tertiary education. Only a couple of holes have been pierced into tertiary education's entrance door by piecemeal reforms. The flows into tertiary education from other tributaries than the "Gymnasium" are still meagre ones and guarantee that the distribution of opportunities retains elements of a corporative society. If socially segregated general education provisions and the modernized *Beruf* concept are sufficient adaptations to modern requirements will be discussed later.

The Beruf: Some Cultivation Implications,
Prospects and Backgrounds

Curriculum, Didactics and Socialization; Workers' "Social Space"

Beruf as the guiding training principle of German apprenticeships includes a curriculum and a didactic dimension, both relevant for the generation of skilled workers' "social space". *Beruf* is something serious, a no-nonsense concept which includes a very sober orientation towards economically relevant practice and the term still includes undertones of "ethical duties and responsibilities" to produce products and services according to "state of the art" quality criteria: "Qualität ist das Anständige" (Th. Heuss; roughly "quality is decent"). It implies that one cannot learn a *Beruf* simply in vocational schools outside the need to perform "when it counts", namely in real life and, more precisely, in working life in a company or institution. Schools, and even good vocational schools, easily become perceived in this vein as "out of touch with reality", "theoretically biased" or "alien to life".

The "production" of vocational skills and competences became the task of a new branch of the education systems at the end of the 19th century in industrially advanced countries, namely vocational education, hence in technical or vocational schools. Not so in Germany. The task of making people vocationally competent and skilled became grafted on economic matters: a mono-integrated training system of the private sector, not a multi-integrated system under public control (see: M. Archer, 1979). Apprenticeships, already in decay, the supply of which by far exceeded the demand (see: H.-W. Schmuhl, 2003, S. 45/46), became politically revitalized by two legal initiatives in 1897 (Handwerkerschutzgesetz) and 1908 (Novelle zur Gewerbeordnung) which tried to "protect" the crafts – a misleading term, because their "dynamisation" was the main intention – by self-help activities supported by government and by the stipulation that only those master craftsmen were allowed to train apprentices, who had passed a master craftsman's examination before a chamber of the crafts.

Thus, youngsters of humble social origins became subject to authoritarian and socially divisive forms of "education" *outside the genuine education system.* In the legal initiatives conceptual vestiges are to be found similar to ideas developed by economists like K. Buecher and G. Schmoller and engineers like the famous locomotive designer R. Garbe. Schmoller held the opinion that it was necessary to find ways and means of governmental regulation of apprenticeships because of its far-reaching disruption. He also found that some parents had contributed to the degeneration of apprenticeships because of their interest to make their children earn money early in life (e.g. by making them accept work in industries instead of undergoing a lower paid apprenticeship). In the interest of future national production, the ethical idea of education had to interfere with present production and to transform it in such a way, which would enable human and occupational education.

Schmoller's idea that the young generation's right on education was more important than the idea of economic freedom was linked to the thought of a revival of the guilds, which he addressed in the wording that a "firm institution with a firm tradition" is needed. There is not much novelty in Schmoller's concept except the reasons. The integration of people of the same trade in a guild was not demanded for economic, but for reasons of the education of the young generation. The ethical idea of an obligation of the older generation to influence the moral development of the younger generation is Schmoller's central idea for the re-consolidation of the guilds.

Robert Garbe, the designer of many successful German locomotives in the end of the 19th/beginning of the 20th century, and in the same time a leading conceptionist of vocational training, developed the basic forms of modern German training in training workshops. He reported proudly in 1888, after a decade of training work, that the idea was firmly established "that a well-managed apprenticeship system is the most powerful lever for the necessary upswing of the trades." (quoted from H. Abel, 1963, S. 34) His training system was clearly linked to *normative* qualifications. In his own words: "To keep a tight rein on the apprentices and to take care of their moral education is always the most important goal of training." H.-U. Wehler concludes: "It is institutions which in the long run guarantee the internalization and acceptance of political authority. ... Because of the fundamental importance of this type of institutionalized control of behaviour, which, to put it briefly, preferred control by others to the encouragement of personal responsibility, we can also discern a structural antipathy to democracy as being one of its most important consequences. This antipathy was certainly one more feature of Germany's social history during the time of the Empire." (H.-U. Wehler, 1997, p. 100)

Everyday training routine in the end of the 19th century/beginning of the 20th century is vividly described in the following report: "The handling of the file, the hammer and the chisel belong to the first exercises. The apprentice gets a bigger irregularly shaped piece of wrought iron, which he has to transform in an exactly shaped cube. With this seemingly simple task all the fundamental skills of vice work can be excellently trained and the most important files and chisels can be used. Till all the six faces of a cube are positioned in a right angle to each other and with a sharp edge, are of the same size and even as they should be, the originally big iron cube becomes smaller and smaller, the wrist more and more supple, the eye sharper and many drops of sweat and sometimes even of blood have to be spilled, because, as the fitter is used to say, 'the lazy flesh must get off the hands'." (quoted from: W. Georg/A. Kunze, 1981, S. 57) The present-day reader may get the impression that the filing exercise, fundamental in German training till many years after World War II, was as much about manual skills and shaping metal cubes, as about shaping characters. In the language of the Nazis "iron educates": the heading of their fundamental training course in metalworking. Not always without irony iron was sometimes called "the most German of all materials", teaching "hardness", also against oneself, obedience, perseverance, to bear physical and mental pains and "to succeed", whatever "the costs" incurred may include, do or die. The hidden curriculum of such drill, besides training real skills, could include an occasional or frequent dwarfing of apprentices in the presence of the experts, journeymen and master craftsmen: "Lehrjahre sind keine Herrenjahre" ("life is not easy at the bottom").

Little by little, vocational schools were added to the apprenticeship procedures, but only as a rather complementary, not as an independent element. They were always an appendix to processes dominated by apprenticeships and should become the place were "systematic" learning could be added to casuistic learning in the company. Unfortunately, the time frame at the vocational school's disposal was rather limited and normally did not exceed 8 hours per week. Prussian 16 hours experiments were not sustainable.

Apprenticeships and the *Beruf* offered Germans of humble (often in technical fields) or middle-level social origins (often in clerical fields) a particular "social space" in case they underwent rigid forms of work education, above unskilled workers, but segregated from academics. They could not climb up to higher echelons, and they could not be reached by the unskilled. The delivery system for *Beruf* competence, the "dual system", in official statements and diagrams is placed on the upper secondary level, but, it does not allow direct transition into the tertiary education phase, which is only possible when time-consuming deviation routes are taken and the "Abitur" threshold is somehow passed. These routes still have a filter effect, as was shown by E. Middendorf (2002) several years ago, but they are a matter of concern since decades (see: S. Grimm 1966).

The extremely early streaming of German pupils in the age of ten to three tracks (Hauptschule, Realschule, Gymnasium) – the "Gesamtschule" is a more recent addendum and does not fundamentally change the three-track structure – plays a major role in "shoveling" youngsters into apprenticeship tracks, a configuration which emerged in the 19th century and unfortunately was confirmed by the "Reichsschulkonferenz" in 1920 and vigorously defended throughout the "Weimar Republic" ("the republic without republicans"). That the Nazis did not submit such a rigid system to democratic reform cannot come as a surprise.

Skilled workers trained in apprenticeships geared towards a *Beruf*, acquire a special status clearly separate from higher positions requiring academic training. They were offered particular employment chances, a relatively elevated wage level, a certain durability of employment and limited career patterns (Meister, technician, instructor) *not accessible* for people with academic qualifications or unskilled workers. Hence, there was "social space" for German skilled workers, in traditional as well as in more modern areas of complex production processes. *Beruf*, thus, still maintained the old guild concept to limit competition and to draw clear borderlines between the different areas of competence. Even people with the highest levels of intellectual skills could be excluded from being a candidate for a certain work position if he/she had been qualified in a different mode not under the "jurisdiction" of companies and chambers, the guilds' present-day successors. They were not regarded as "experienced" and therefore "incompetent". It is evident that such borderlines cause rigidities in modern production and that is why recent industrial *Beruf* concepts are designed in overlapping fashion and should include "key qualifications". In the crafts sector older concepts still can be distinctly different.

Such social space is largely generated – besides the curriculum differences between general education curricula and "training ordinances" – by "practice" in companies, "practical experience" in production and distribution and, not least, the "social experience" related to such practice. This kind of "experience" creates a difference to people who have "only" attended school and even to those people who have attended a very "high" school, namely the university – differences not only in the curriculum, but also in the socialization dimension.

The observation of the didactical principle of "practice-orientation" means apprenticeship in the rough and tumble of the workplace, in a situation "when it counts", and not in the "protected" area of a school. It is of the utmost importance for generating the social space German skilled workers inhabit: certainly a very stern didactical principle indeed, with an enormous influence on shaping personality and character. Not very well-meaning observers might be inclined to comment: "hard, obedient, narrow-minded, with stamina" (isn't that the image a certain genre of war movies disseminates with pleasure?). Capacities to ride roughshod over personal characteristics were enshrined in traditional apprenticeships and, thus, they are very different from what nowadays is regarded as good didactics. But, such facts were consciously included in their re-vitalization. The differentiating criterion has proved to be very hard indeed and skilled workers' social space rarely could be "invaded" by people of a different kind of competences, even in those cases, which were described as "superior". "Überqualifiziert" (too competent) was and is the typical term with which this social space for skilled workers is defended.

The workers social space is generated by company-based training (instead of school-based education) and, thus, by a company-based socialization as well and there is a whole workingmen's culture generating and telling sarcastic jokes about the incompetence of people qualified in other ways in the manner of "five times cut off and still too short" ("fünfmal abgeschnitten und immer noch zu kurz"): a culture which helps them defend their "inherited" social space. German skilled workers "graduate" by a particular "rite of passage", which makes them different from low skilled workers and people qualified in institutional arrangements including tertiary education institutions: universities and "Fachhochschulen" (for starkly contrasting perceptions of company-based socialization in German training, see: K. Abraham, 1953, especially pp. 69 -76 ; H. Kern, 1975).

Apprentices in their training and socialization period (apprenticeships) are integrated into "communities" of skilled men (girls and women were rarely included in technical fields), normally led by a "Meister" or an "Ausbilder" (in industries) and consisting of journeymen (skilled workers in industries) and themselves, the apprentices, who are on the lowest level of such communities. "Integration" may have been "easier" during the first decade after World War II, when workers often lived in fairly closed social "milieus" and settlements, while such milieus seem to be less sharply segregated nowadays. But, this is, admittedly, a superficial impression, while social differences certainly have grown again in recent years. Apprentices learn a wide variety of very different matters, namely:

- that it is wise to follow the more experienced persons, because they have mastered the "tricks of the trade"
- to follow the business needs of a company (*very different from following a school curriculum or the wishes of teachers, not least, if the theory is right that "tasks" shape consciousness, especially of relatively young persons*)
- technical expertise according to national training standards
- "probieren geht über studieren!" (the proof of the pudding is in the eating): The German wording includes a particular meaning which should not remain unnoticed: trying (practically) has more worth than theoretical studies!
- insights into the world of work and the life of adults
- to obey to commands, to respect "authority" or, to use youthful slang, to know "wo der Hammer hängt" (to know where the hammer is kept – actually, to know *who* has the hammer, who has the power)
- to carefully scrutinize the opinions of non-members (non-members of the trade, outsiders) of the community for all implications imaginable
- maybe even to hold the opinions of non-members of the vocational community in low esteem or even in contempt.

Learning in a world designed for a temporary period of learning is certainly different from learning in a world designed for earning one's livelihood: a need, which regularly lasts much longer than schooling. The rough and tumble of the work place usually teaches something different than school education and this is no German particularity. The German particularity "only" consists of the fact, that much larger numbers of young people of relatively tender age were trained and socialized in the context of companies compared to other countries of the European Union (please mind, that many of them were 14 years of age in the first decades after World War II, when they started their apprenticeships). Compared to countries with early school-leaving age and no apprenticeship systems in place, this can be regarded as a (productive) advantage. Compared to countries with later (full-time) school-leaving age and less educational tracking things may have been different. Unfortunately, one cannot be sure, that the kind of practice-oriented technical shrewdness plus the equally shrewd observation and utilization of power relations, included in the German way of company-based competence development represents an internationally appreciated level of social accomplishment, civic refinement and intercultural sophistication though products and economic outcomes are widely acclaimed still. Youthful minds are receptive and learning in strongly hierarchical conditions produces different outcomes from educational institutions, which are certainly no "islands of the blessed" either. Especially in situations of crises and emergencies German intellectuals have been sometimes painfully aware of the different consequences of different socializations, even in those cases in which an apologetic stand was taken (see for instance: M. Scheler, 1917, S. 100/101).

*Quality of Apprenticeship Training;
Prospects of Apprenticeship Training (training for a Beruf)*

Mass apprenticeship "systems" in economically advanced countries are chameleons offering highly modern and advanced learning conditions to some apprentices, but by far not for all. Small and medium-sized companies often (not always) operate on lower technological levels and learning might be dependent on the unforeseeable flow of customer orders, which do not include work tasks in pedagogically structured sequences. In addition, in medium-sized companies, the problem can arise that companies are too small to have a separate training department with well-trained instructors and training managers, while they are too big to facilitate intensive contacts between the apprentices and the personnel officially in charge of training. In such cases, apprentices still might be nothing else than helpers, and their training might oscillate between training and work, in some cases with an emphasis on work, in other cases with an emphasis on learning. Then, with their competence increasing, they grow gradually into the work tasks of the more experienced workers. The actual instructors are not always well qualified because pedagogically unskilled and untrained journeymen or skilled workers might be involved. In such cases the major rule for apprentices' learning processes seems to be: to participate, in one way or another, in what has to be done from an economic point of view (see: M. Leidner, 2001, especially S. 186 – 201).

Apprenticeships in advanced areas and companies can be future-oriented, on high quality levels and include more than what is officially required (German training standards are minimum standards), while others might be grafted onto traditional and even outdated methods and techniques. Thus, even in advanced economies, the quality level, the future relevance (hence the job security in the trades to be learned), the wage levels, the competency and quality of instructors, the overall pedagogical or instructional quality of apprenticeships are usually very uneven and their capacity to provide smooth transitions to "the educational mainstream" is far from guaranteed.

In the contrary, the retention effect of apprenticeships separated by deep grooves and trenches from the genuinely educational provisions were consciously used in the revitalization of apprenticeships in the end of the 19th and the beginning of the 20th century and the same applies to Kerschensteiner's concepts (see below). While his pedagogical ideas are not fashionable any more in the pedagogical profession, his and the concepts of other educationists and educational politicians are still enshrined in the organizational features of the German education and training arrangement and still have an effect on the underlying pedagogical assumptions. In addition, Kerschensteiner's ideas, in a subterranean way, pop up every now and then, which shows that they have become part of the German collective memory and how educational problems are "instinctively" approached (see: M. Miegel, 2002, S. 140 – 145), usually without comparative efforts.

Be it as it may, from an economic point of view it is food for thought that the formerly wide range of internationally competitive sectors of the German economy has been considerably narrowed by international competition, not least in camera industries, watch making, shipbuilding, garment and leather processing industries, pharmaceutical industries, entertainment electronics etc. and that disappearing or diminished sectors have not sufficiently been counterbalanced by newly emerging sectors or the revitalization of older ones. This, at least, is what the unemployment statistics tell. Mass apprenticeship "systems" are related to *present* economic practice, not so much to newly emerging sectors and technologies, which either require deliberate promotion by governmental policies or the know-how of and the risk-taking by private entrepreneurs, who then would need to be equipped with innovative technological and other skills not trainable by already existing technologies. Therefore, self-administered apprenticeships have a strong practice-oriented side, but also a weak future orientation, especially when "big technological leaps" are in the offing.

Certainly, concerning the transformation of raw material into final products the traditional German training system made sure that apprentices, journeymen and "Meisters" "travelled" on the road from theory to practice and from practice to theory many times and that they carefully honed and refined their skills and competences in many such loops. The performance profile of such workers was embossed by careful and reliable application of acquired competences, especially and traditionally in the area of manual activities to be supported by a degree of theoretical knowledge. When the engineers designed a new machine, the skilled workers (tool and dye and mould makers) translated the design into metal and the engineers were interested to listen to the skilled workers' reports of outcomes (especially to the workers responsible for putting the machine into operation in the customer's premises) and of clients' comments in order to refine their designs. Such a concept usually implies slow and steady (not revolutionary) improvement of products.

Berufe, generated in practice-oriented apprenticeships, contributed to German productivity and high product quality for several decades.

But there is rarely something perfect in this world and the same applies to apprenticeships and *Beruf*. Occupations became more and more cognitive over the years and decades and there are limitations to instil the required competences by the traditional form of apprenticeships usually based on the lower general education tracks (the combination of Vocational Academies or "Fachhochschulen" and company-based training are different matters).

Apprenticeships and the "Beruf" concept based on them do not fit smoothly into the overall education system and are co-responsible for the "shoveling" of youngsters into lower education tracks. In addition, the grooves, gaps and trenches of the German education and training "system" are likely to have repercussions in the world of work. It is not likely that advanced production concepts developed and implemented in other countries are always fully applicable in German companies (e.g. knowledge sharing): It does not look like a coherent or consistent policy, when German companies try to borrow "production" and "management concepts", while their educational underpinnings are purposefully overlooked. The recent discussion of German PISA results, focusing on "performance"- or "achievement"-related topics seem to bypass other essential effects of such grooves, gaps, and trenches on German economic performance like social attitudes, co-operation capacity, general and social responsibility, etc.

W.-D. Greinert (2003, S. 8) several years ago, analysed what he called the "bi-polar structure" of the German education and training arrangement, while M. Baethge, H. Solga and M. Wieck recently spoke of the "German educational schism" (2007, S. 16), which is generated by the following facts and processes: "For the German Education system as a whole the institutional separation between higher general education (Gymnasia and universities) and vocational education is fundamental. Both big educational areas follow different institutional orders (Ordnungen); which means: they are regulated according to different political order principles, they are differently financed, they follow different goals or fulfil different functions, which have effects on the design of the learning and training processes in all dimensions (…)." (S. 16)

Summarizing such findings it seems to be adequate to speak of German education and training taking place in a culturally and socially divisive arrangement in which one belongs to educational "high culture", the other one to educational "low culture" ascribing their respective "graduates" different lifetime earnings and different social and life chances, notwithstanding their innate talents and capabilities: educational worlds apart. While "Beruf" and apprenticeships can be perceived – not without reason – as two of the major causes of several decades of German economic achievement, their institutional arrangements are educationally and politically doubtful, because they contribute to stable educational and social inequalities between citizens and therefore are responsible for rigidities, which hamper the educational and social flexibility and mobility of Germans. They also limit horizontal and vertical cooperation in the work place or make it more difficult, more prone to disturbances and on lower levels of continuous improvement than production concepts underpinned by more egalitarian and inclusive education and training "systems", whether they are based on western equal-opportunity-considerations or eastern considerations of "harmony" and "homogeneity".

In addition, the decision-making arrangements place curriculum decisions in training outside of parliamentary or ministerial control, thus, largely beyond the reach of the voters. Germany is a parliamentary democracy, but, because of such mechanisms, a reduced one, as far as education and training are concerned. Unfortunately, it cannot be excluded that there are spill-over effects, which also affect other areas. Other reduction effects are also built-in in the German political "system" as described in the earlier sections of this paper. In the reduced democracy the balance between the political weight of citizens and the weight of the trustees of their votes, the parliamentary parties, has been strongly tipped in favour of the latter. The imbalances between the parties and "the sovereign", the citizens, have reached serious proportions of citizens' disenfranchisement, which can have repercussions in the long run, if they are not redressed.

Historical Aspects of German Education and Beruf *Training:*
Kerschensteiner and some consequences of his concepts

It is hardly possible to understand the historical development of German apprenticeships aiming for a *Beruf* and the German general education "system" without an analysis of Georg Kerschensteiner's educational concepts, although they are several decades, and some of them even more than hundred years old. But, explanations of Kerschensteiner's views and concepts are confronted with serious problems, not least with many research desiderata. An exhaustive description and analysis of Kerschensteiner's views and concepts is far beyond the frame of a paper like this, especially because:

1. Research work concerning Kerschensteiner is still too patchy. There is no edition of his writings, speeches and letters available, satisfying scientific needs. The existing ones don't promote a historical-critical understanding of Kerschensteiner's work. They are selective and do not offer access to the roots and the development of his thoughts. In the available editions, the reader encounters rather profound difficulties to recognize, how Kerschensteiner's concepts are "embedded" in the political and intellectual situation of his lifetime. His writings were published in many editions and texts were often several times reworked which makes it difficult to identify the original "messages" and intentions and the reasons why and how they were reworked. This is especially important in the case of an author who adhered to the "indirect method" (Dr. Neuhaus, Verwaltungsbericht 1912, S. 42, quoted from: H.-P. Bruchhäuser, 2000, S. 500, footnote 6), rather tactical education approaches aiming for goals, which should not be discovered by the "clients" of that education: "1. It is impossible to lure trout with cherry stones; 2. but when the cherry stone is covered by a grasshopper, the trout will devour it together with the cherry stone, … .That is the reason why in Munich we have introduced workshops into the school; they are the grasshoppers, with which we catch the trout. But they are not the goal, but the means of our educational intention." (op. cit., S. 500, footnote 3).

2. There is also no scientific biography available and the ones available serve hagiographic purposes.

3. In addition, there is also no comprehensive history of modern vocational education and training in Germany available, but only analyses of particular topics, aspects and periods of German training and the threefold unavailability (no scientific edition of Kerschensteiner's works; no scientific biography; no comprehensive history of modern German training) does not allow a "minimum certainty" in the assessment of his work.

4. Kerschensteiner lived and worked in troubled times (before and after World War I – "the prime catastrophe of the 20th century" – and during the ascendance of fascism in Germany), and to relate his thinking to other educationists, like Herbart, Pestalozzi and Dewey, who lived either in different periods of time or in different political and cultural contexts, is clearly insufficient. By education he was mathematician and natural scientist (including some biological studies), so that, because of obvious reasons, strong interests in Darwin's theories of natural evolution and other biological theories in Darwin's wake are likely. The strong traces of social-organological, Darwinist and Social Darwinist (Spencerian) thinking in his concepts therefore are not surprising, but their origins need to be identified (Albert Schaeffle, Gregor Mendel, August Weismann, Ernst Haeckel, Otto Amonn, etc.); e.s.g., it should not be overlooked that Ernst Haeckel, the most prominent German follower of Darwin, had a wide audience for his books during Kerschensteiner's lifetime. Also pan-psychic currents in the wake of Eduard von Hartmann's "Philosophie des Unbewussten" (Philosophy of the Unconscious) may have played a role in the development of Kerschensteiner's pedagogical concepts, because von Hartmann's philosophy ("the purposeful effects of the educational instinct") was enormously popular among German and French intellectuals in the end of the 19th century and there are references to von Hartmann in Kerschensteiner's writings (see for instance: G. Kerschensteiner, 1917, S. 12). While such references are rather vague, those to Ernst Haeckel's thoughts are more substantial. It could well be that either Ernst Haeckel's or Eduard von Hartmann's thoughts (or those of both men) are echoed in one of Kerschensteiner's poems, reported by his wife and by Th. Wilhelm, a propagandist of the holocaust who made a brilliant academic career in post-war Germany. (see: M. Kerschensteiner, 1939, S. 165; Th. Wilhelm, 1957). The poem reports "iron laws" "effective through space and time" from which no human being can liberate himself/herself and its statement seems to be very close to the world of ideas E. Haeckel had unfolded in several of his publications: evolutionary theory transformed into "the laws of the world process", in which the "subjective factor" or "human will" had no role to play (see for instance: E. Haeckel, 1984, S. 186f.). Is this the

background why "Sachlichkeit" became "Sittlichkeit" for Kerschensteiner? Also Otto Amonn's writings had a wide circulation in the end of the 19th and the beginning of the 20th century and there are terminological and other similarities between Amonn and Kerschensteiner, which need to be clarified (for instance concerning the "usefulness" (Brauchbarkeit) of citizens). There is also a certain similarity between the educational concepts developed by Albert Schaeffle, the foremost German social-organological thinker of the 19th century, and the concepts developed by Kerschensteiner. The linkage between Kerschensteiner's educational concepts and those of E. Spranger, who was a decided adversary of the "Weimar Republic", is known. To cut a long argument short: Kerschensteiner needs to be understood in the intellectual situation of his time and not simply as the German Dewey or as "Pestalozzi's heir" (Spranger). An attempt to address such a complex topic in a paper like this, while research on Kerschensteiner is lacking, would be much too daring.

5. Many attempts have been made to put a label upon Kerschensteiner's work, but as long as research about Kerschensteiner is as patchy as it is, such attempts are not extremely solid, but play with fire. While some called him "liberal", "pragmatic", "democrat", "democrat from the beginning", "realist", others have called his concepts "a miserable hypocrisy" (H. Schulz) or have pointed to the fact that the Nazis called him "a road paver of national-socialist education" (J. Schwarzfischer), hence evaluative verdicts could not be more contradictory and assessments in the present research situation necessarily have an air of arbitrariness, although many ingredients of his concepts are known, which are no paragons of democratic virtue.

Therefore, in this paper, Kerschensteiner's thinking shall be explained by a number of basic statements in need of more analytical efforts, focusing on terms essential in Kerschensteiner's theories, not least in his concept of "staatsbürgerliche Erziehung" (literally: the education of state citizens) and his political party affiliation, while he was member of the German "Reichstag". It is hoped that they are less controversial than "final" assessments and labels. A couple of considerations will be added concerning Kerschensteiner's enduring influence on German educational structures and policies:

1. The term "the state" vacillates. It is not "the government" of the Anglo-Saxon tradition. "The state" as "an organic whole" is, on the one hand, a kind of a summary, embodiment and apex of "the whole" of the "social body", but in a purified form, and as such separate from the "social body" and more ethical than the "social body" ever could be. In this sense the "state body" is beyond the clashes of narrow social interests or beyond the conflicts of daily life, but represents the higher and nobler interests of society. This is the aspect in which Hegel's state perception seems to resonate. On the other hand "the state" integrates the "social body" (or is identical with it; compare E. Haeckel, 1984, S. 19, borrowing Schaeffle's book title "Bau und Leben des socialen Körpers"); it is an organic whole which is thought to be a "fuller" or "richer" concept, than what "mechanistic democracy" indicates, which is not supposed to fit well to Germany (see: E. Troeltsch 1915, S. 52 – 90; E. Troeltsch 1966 (reprint from 1924), S. 52). Ernst Troeltsch expressed convictions widerspread among German "liberals" in that period of time, and Kerschensteiner belonged to a liberal political party ("Fortschrittliche Volkspartei"). His religious believes were not religious in the strict sense, but certainly more of Haeckel's kind who mystified and deified natural laws, causing the development of life in steps from non-organic to organic stages. "The state" and "social body" in this sense is a functional structure in which no "organ" (including the "Staatsbürger") can change position. All the "Staatsbürger" must play their – by nature – different roles, thus becoming "useful (brauchbare) members" of the "state" or the "social body". In Ernst Haeckel's following the claim became fashionable that the new cellular theory would have proved subordination as the principal law of organic nature, which can be traced back to Haeckel himself (E. Haeckel, 1984, S. 203) Every cell, even when autonomous, would be subject to the body as a whole: The "scientific" rejection of democracy became an intellectual sport in Germany. In many aspects Haeckel's views have a certain similarity with Kerschensteiner's and the prior certainly was influential on the development of the ladder's thoughts, but "how" and in which elements, is not clear. But, one should be aware that Haeckel's legacy is a rather mixed blessing (see: E. Haeckel, 1906, chapter 17) and includes a considerable amount of social and eth-

nical racism. "The differences between the highest and the lowest persons are bigger than those between the lowest persons and the highest animals."

2. The "Staatsbürger" (state citizen) is also not the "citizen" of the Anglo-Saxon tradition and consequently "staatsbürgerliche Erziehung" is not identical with "civic education", but rather the opposite. The "state citizen" is a limb of the state, hence a subject of "the whole". The "state citizens" are as different as "the worm is different from the eagle", because of the "different qualities of their souls" and because of the existence of different "Lebensformen" (forms of life) according to Eduard Spranger's concept, which became essential for Kerschensteiner. The "state citizens" only superficially belong to the same species *homo sapiens*, while their inward qualities are *fundamentally* different. The different qualities of their souls can be traced back to the different genetic make-up of the "state citizens", while the "social pyramid" is more or less a "natural pyramid". There seems to be a pre-stabilized harmony between the "structures of the souls" and labour market structures and requirements.

3. "The state" is involved in a struggle for existence with other species of "the state". The German "state" is a "state of culture and of law" and the unique cultural expression of the particular nature of her people, hence, extremely precious.

4. "Staatsbürgerliche Erziehung" cannot be the same kind of "general education" for everybody, but must be "vocational education" according to the different "psychic equipments" of the "Staatsbürger". A. Siemsen called Kerschensteiner's opinion "democratic", while F. K. Ringer even thought Kerschensteiner's demand to educate everybody according to his talents to be "unusually democratic" (F. K. Ringer, 1990, p. 270). Such an understanding reads more conventional liberalism into Kerschensteiner's thinking than there truly was, because Kerschensteiner's position is based upon "all men are *not* created equal" and therefore everybody has to be educated to become a "useful" citizen in different kinds of vocational education according to the different qualities of their souls. There is a considerable amount of evidence in Kerschensteiner's writings that his educational concepts and political imaginations followed the basic concept of an "order of inequality".

5. "Beruf" is essential in order to structure the "social body" and it mirrors the different giftedness of the individuals. While the "psychic quality" of the "Staatsbürger" is finely graded, it can be categorized into two big groups, those "theoretically gifted" and those "practically gifted". The latter group has to be educated and trained in vocational schools for the "handarbeitende" (manually working) parts of the population. Consequently, "general education" is an illusion, as every individual can only be educated according to the qualities of his/her soul, to which education must correspond partially or totally, while many parents are by far too ambitious by sending their children to schools beyond the children's capacities.

6. Kerschensteiner's distinctions between those "practically gifted" and those "theoretically gifted" and between citizens "equipped" with different "soul qualities" has not only educational but also political consequences: A) Those "practically gifted" have to be "educated", trained, and constantly "habituated" to be prepared to offer their services, not according to their own will, but according to the will of others. B) "The upper strata of society are and will remain the educators of the people" ("Die oberen Stände sind und bleiben die Erzieher des Volkes" (G. Wehle (Hg.): Kerschensteiner, 1966, S. 87). C) "Only few of our compatriots ("Volksgenossen") are capable to develop a firm opinion about the purpose of the state and its means. Most of them have to leave it to others, to think politically for them, and the direction of their "staatsbürgerliche" activities and their political opinions remain eternally the effects of the bigger or smaller suggestive power, which the leaders and their promises exert on them." (G. Kerschensteiner, quoted from Kw. Stratmann, 1999, S. 635)

7. Some citizens are useful, some are useless and the limit of usefulness divides the "weakly gifted persons" (see: O. Amonn, 1900, S. 61, diagram 2); also in Amonn's case the relation between his approach and Kerschensteiner's is unclear; but the similarity between both approaches is striking. As far as can be seen, Kerschensteiner did *not* radicalize such views. But, one should be aware that they became the jumping board for barbarous approaches under the label "lebensunwertes Leben".

8. There is a remarkably strong anti-democratic and anti-western strain in Kerschensteiner's concepts, which does not justify the term "lib-

eralism" in the conventional sense. Kerschensteiner's "liberalism" is underpinned by social-darwinist and other currents, widespread in Germany at that period of time in all social sciences and in philosophy (for the "völkisch" and other rightist varieties, see: A. Kolnai, 1938), which justifies the paradoxical expressions, that his "liberalism" was an "illiberal" or "authoritarian liberalism". In the German case the application of the term "liberalism" is doubtful for Kerschensteiner's lifetime, when the contents of such "liberalism" are not explained. "Liberalism" for that period of time is a cloak of many colours and has no sufficient selectivity.

Kerschensteiner's continuous importance for German education and training consists in the fact, that the "organic" structuring of the education and training sector – essential in his concept – could not be overcome (see: M. Kraul, 1984, S. 168/169). The corporatist (berufsständische) structural imaginations, which dominated education, were still summarized by the "Deutscher Ausschuss fuer das Bildungs- und Erziehungswesen" (German Committee for Education) at the beginning of the sixties of the last century in the following words: "One strives for the preservation of the present education structure and argues that it would have proven its worth. The three-track structure consisting of higher schools, Volksschulen (people's schools) and middle schools (Realschulen) would correspond to the three main strata of vocations which would have emerged in modern life: an intellectually leading, an executing and an intermediate stratum in between with elevated responsibility. The three-track structure also would do justice to the main three types of giftedness: a theoretical, a practical and a theoretical-practical type." (Quoted from G. Lenhardt. In: H. Joas (Hg.), 2001, S. 325) In the wording chosen by the committee Kerschensteiner's and similar concepts still resonate. Still, as late as 1959, "one of the remaining advocates of eugenics and Social Darwinism, K. V. Mueller, ... declared that 'ability is a biological category' and 'unconditionally rooted in hereditary traits' and that any socio-political measures aimed at changing 'the natural correspondence of school selection and social selection' were futile." (S. Robinsohn/ J. C. Kuhlmann, 1995, S. 26; reprint from 1967).

More or less strong remnants of an "organic" structuring of the social body ("die Gliederung des Volkskörpers") continued to exist from imperial Germany, to the "Weimar Republic", to fascism and to the Federal Republic of Germany, before and after unification: the remnants express themselves in the continuity of the existence of a mass-relevant pre-democratic "Beruf" delivery arrangement and a three-track general education "system". The predominance of "selection" (Auslese) in such a system does not facilitate, alleviate, and encourage education, but limit educational efforts, either according to an interpretation of the students' talents and corresponding tracking, or according to labour market requirements and corresponding prognoses on training needs or both. The non-alleviation and –facilitation of education and the "sorting" of students therefore is a typical feature of the present German education and training arrangement, and German public and private sector educational policies, which necessarily must have consequences in the transition to the knowledge-based society. A division of the educational culture tends to harbour a certain amount of educational complacency and even of contempt for education.

The Role of "Verbände" in Apprenticeship Training

In the Federal Republic of Germany vocational education and training is regulated by a peculiar interplay between formal governmental regulation, social self-administration (by employers' and employees' organizations) and company-based implementation of regulations mainly designed by private sector representatives. Governmental regulation – as already shown – has more or less confirmed the traditional arrangements of the private sector, after far-reaching reform projects were defeated in the seventies: a fact described by some analysts as "a demonstration of political powerlessness and economic power". "Duality" is mainly a phenomenon consisting of the design of training standards in which companies and "Verbände" are involved, the control of the appropriate implementation of such standards by the "Verbände" and the need to rely on companies' willingness to train. In the established "training order" problems arise in newly emerging economic fields, before "Verbände" can be founded.

The companies' orientation at "productivity" and "product quality" - important for their survival - cannot stand much interference from sides alien to the production process, which is sensitive to goals and processes *not* serving such goals. "Verbände" cannot accept training stipulations which cannot be borne by their members or loose their influence. The control of companies' training activities offers some leeway to companies as well as to the "Verbände", for instance, in reflecting a particular company's problem to implement the training regulations properly – a leeway, which governments obliged to keep the norms strictly, usually don't have. Because "Verbände" can only promote, but not guarantee the satisfying implementation of regulations, the criticism of their usefulness is a permanent phenomenon of such a control institute. Governments, on the other hand, usually closely observed by the general public and under various pressures to take different and sometimes contradicting viewpoints into consideration are rarely well placed for the design and pursuit of single-minded "productivity" and "product quality" oriented curricula. And companies, aware of such facts, are not in a position to generate sufficient trust vis-à-vis governmental capacities in such curriculum construction.

Beruf is a company-overarching concept, and, a concept with nation-wide validity, but it needs companies as training providers. It is company-based, but not company-specific. Here the chambers and other private sector organizations (the "Verbände") enter the stage. If they have either been granted the privilege by government, if they have been active in training before government could be interested in the field, or if they have some time, somehow in the history of a country managed to wrestle the privilege from government to be responsible for making the young generation vocationally competent, is not important. But, in any case, companies must *widely*, with as little exception as possible, regard them as their own representatives, flesh from their own flesh, so to speak, then, but only then, company-based training has a chance to become a major undertaking: regarded from the supply-side (which is not a sufficient condition, it needs demand-side complementation).

This requires a governmental concept to be in place, which reflects the history of the society under consideration and normally cannot be developed on the spot just when the need arises or when governmental planners deem it timely to implement such a concept. It has serious implications for any country's balance of power. Such a concept can be functionally efficient, if the country's history allows its implementation, while it is politically questionable in most genuine democracies: it implies a limitation of popular sovereignty and of parliamentary decision-making, as well as of ministerial supervision and influence, hence, the electorate's will and capacity to shape the future of the country.

A *Beruf*, legally valid and accepted by the shareholders of the "dual system" on a nationwide labour market, cannot be designed by individual companies. But, the companies must have a high degree of trust in the training designers. The most secure way to generate trust is the transfer of the design tasks to the private sector's own experts from companies and associations under the inclusion of trade union experts and scientific specialists. This pattern can be found in all the modern training standards published by the BIBB. If we take the training standard for "mechatronics specialists" as an example, the group responsible for the publication of the training standard consisted of: 2 members of the BIBB, 1 member of the industrial association of German machine-tool industry, 1 member of the metal workers trade union, 1 professor from a university, 1 member of the Siemens AG and 1 member of the Audi AG. Scientifically supported design by the private sector's own experts, complemented by trade unions, unimpeded by governmental control and regulation, therefore holds one of the master keys to private sector investment in TVET in Germany.

Outside interference, even from elected government for instance, would not be helpful. A company-overarching training standard (in principle not favouring any existing company) based on the *Beruf*, therefore must be designed by a body which is trusted by companies and therefore the chambers and other representatives from top sector organizations and company experts are the "natural candidates". The inclusion of partisan and non-partisan training experts, a member of the trade unions and a university professor, adds viewpoints to the design which make it more "complete", "well-rounded" and more acceptable for the workers and employees and for the wider public.

Without the institution *Beruf* an understanding of German apprenticeship training is virtually impossible and German apprenticeship training is to be characterized by "self-administration" of the private sector. This aspect makes it different from apprenticeship systems based on individual companies' training activities even though they may take place in big quantities. In other cases, when apprenticeship is based on self-administration of the private sector or branch organizations, self-administration has not gained the same level of governmental appreciation as in Germany (chamber concepts might be different) and/or the population's demand for education/training is fuelled by different education and training imaginations, ideals and goals. The linkage of German apprenticeships to self-administration therefore is an essential element. In the words of Rüdiger Altmann, an author of the German Chambers of Industry and Commerce: apprenticeships "became an elastic structure *based* on self-administration." (R. Altmann, 1961, S. 230; *my emphasis* – K. Sch.) For the German Chambers of Industry and Commerce "self-administration", hence, is a *structural feature* of apprenticeships. Altmann's statement has been met with critical remarks by Kw. Stratmann and M. Schlösser (1992, S. 66), who apparently see it as an exaggeration or otherwise as a mis-judgment. In general, Altmann's position is not liked by authors in favour of "public administration" of training. But, if one likes it or not is another matter. Altmann's statement is a reasonable description of the existing situation of *apprenticeships in Germany* and an explanation, why – as Stratmann/ Schlösser confirm – the German chambers and private sector organizations defend energetically apprenticeships as well as self administration. In addition, the linkage between apprenticeships and self-administration is confirmed by authors directly involved in the design and implementation process of apprenticeship standards without contradiction by other non-partisan authors (see: H. A. Hesse, 1968, S. 114; quoting E. Krause). With Altmann's statement, we are at the roots of the stability and dynamics of German apprenticeships and close to the causes of the size of German apprenticeship provision. The linkage to *self-administration* is in effect a booster for apprenticeships, which can be compared to the function of a turbocharger in a car. But, this turbocharger hardly allows installation like a spare-part in other political cultures, which do not accept private sector organizations to play a public role.

The Duisburg university professor for vocational education, G. Kutscha, analyzes the problem of the insertion of German training in the German political frame in the following words: "This implies also, that the state (government) has to hand over political competences to "private government" of the corporations and has to generate incentives for cooperation. The implied authorization problem in its core concerns the normative contents of the democratic state and the legitimacy of her institutions, parliaments in particular, in the process of the production of collectively binding decisions (see Offe 1984). The argument is not easily to be rejected, that corporative arrangements devalue constitutionally and legally authorized decision-making bodies and bypass their responsibility ("dominance of the associations"). (G. Kutscha 1997, S. 672; *my translation* – K. Sch.).

The wide-spread understanding of the *Berufe* as "governmentally regulated task fields in the employment system" (see for instance a text selected by random choice: F. Rauner/G. Spoettl, 2002, S. 81) ignores and omits the substantial role of private sector organizations and, therefore, is not satisfying and paints the design and construction of *Berufe* in more democratic colours than the process deserves. German ministries rubber-stamp the drafts of new training standards into "state-recognized training ordinances" and they are – especially in the case of crafts vocations – a kind of chaperons, who observe "the decency" of the drafts, or if they interfere with other vocations' inherited competence claims. The design as such is essentially left to the "social partners".

The Situation after World War II:
The Renewal of the "Ordnungsarbeit" of the "Verbände"

According to H. Benner and H. Schmidt "the continuity and the further development of governmental activities with respect to the structure of dual vocational training after World War II", can be traced back to Paul Ziertmann, a ministerial official dismissed by the Nazis, re-employed by British occupational forces in the "Zentralamt für Wirtschaft" in Minden/Westphalia. With the edition of an ordinance on December 30th, 1946, on "the recognition, the change and the nullification of "Lehr- und Anlernberufen" etc. the task of the authority was described, in order "to secure the necessary uniformity in the vocational training of the upcoming generation in the trades." (see: H. Benner/H. Schmidt, 1994, S. 7/8) In this document the structures are described, which since 1969 (Federal Vocational Training Act) are characteristic for the cooperation of government and the "social partners".

73

A little bit later the "Chambers of Industry and Commerce" founded two "Arbeitsstellen" "in order to avoid a dangerous vacuum" in 1947 (E. Krause, 1970, quoted from Hilbert, J., 1990, p. 27). They were attached to the Dortmund IHK, responsible for technical training, the other one attached to the Muenchen IHK, responsible for commercial training. Two years later the German Chambers of Industry and Commerce, the "Bundesverband der Deutschen Industrie (BDI)" and the "Bundesvereinigung der Deutschen Arbeitgeberverbände (BDA)" together founded the "Arbeitsstelle für Betriebliche Berufsbildung (ABB)". Financing was covered by the German Chambers (50%) and the BDI and the BDA (25% each).

The ABB jumped into "a vacuum" understanding herself as the de-facto follow-up institute of the former "Imperial Institute for Vocational Training". But, the ABB's competence was more limited, as it did not cover the crafts sector. Besides empirically-founded order policy (called "Ordnungsarbeit"), including company visits, surveys, experts' conversations, work of specialized committees, the ABB was responsible from 1965 for scientific work analyses.

The procedure employed for the acknowledgement of the training vocations (trainee occupations) included up to this point drafts of various "Ordnungsmitteln". They were discussed in an experts' committee consisting of instructors, chamber representatives, representatives of branch organizations, representatives of trade unions and vocational school teachers. If the representatives reached an agreement, it became the "task" of the German Chambers, the BDI and the BDA to decide if they could agree also. Subsequently the draft was submitted to the Ministry of Economic Affairs for acknowledgement. The Federal Ministry of Economic Affairs, after consultation with the Ministry of Labour, rubber-stamped the new training ordinance into a "state-recognized training ordinance". The ordinance became compulsory by including the "Berufsbild" (basically the essence of the training ordinance) into the apprenticeship contract. This procedure was modernized by the Vocational Training Act 1969, but in essence is also valid under the new conditions: the ABB is replaced by the BIBB and the Federal Ministry of Labour is replaced by the Federal Ministry of Education and Science. There are a couple of other changes, but essentially, the procedure is very similar.

The Political and Educational Embeddedness of the "Dual System" – A Brief Summary of Major Boosting Effects on the Demand and the Supply-Side

The Demand-Side Booster of Apprenticeships
(the three-track general education "system")

Several years ago, the well-known German training expert, Prof. W.-D. Greinert, published his analysis "Realistic Education in Germany" (2003). According to Greinert "the German educational particularity has arrived at its final destination; a completely different model of organization and control of school, vocational training and scientific studies is in demand, …" (preface, S. XI). Greinert holds the view, that "the German education system is different from the international standard because there is, on the one hand, a three- or four-track structure in lower secondary education (Hauptschule, Realschule, Gymnasium and Gesamtschule), on the other hand, a sharp separation between the "general" and the "vocational" institutions in upper secondary education. Without doubt these peculiarities are a policy burden from the 19th century, which obviously diminishes the performance capabilities of the general school and of vocational training in Germany in a massive way" (W.-D. Greinert, 2003, S. 1).

If there is something like an international standard, does this standard imply – among other aspects – that "a sharp separation between the "general" and the "vocational" institutions in upper secondary education" is avoided? And what does it mean, that it is *not* avoided in Germany? Greinert himself points to the following: "a policy burden from the 19th century". In the German case the gap between "general" and "vocational" dates back to pre-democratic times, which could not be overcome even after nearly 60 years of democracy.

This paper agrees with Greinert's view, that the "dual system" cannot be explained just by an analysis of training itself, but only, if one places the "dual" training track into the wider environment of the particular German general education arrangement and if one recognizes the affiliations with the economic as well as the political system: an embeddedness which, by the way, makes the "systemic" view in Luhmann's footsteps (the "dual system" as a separate – "ausdifferenziertes" – "system") a rather doubtful perspective.

The still superior numerical intake of German apprenticeships, compared with those of most other economically advanced countries, is not simply produced by the apprenticeship "system" itself or by cultural values (although they play an important role), but to a large extent by a general education "system", which was subject to conservation policies, preserving a traditional multi-track educational structure. It includes strong social tracking processes and is different from the education "systems" of other European nations, which have merged different tracks or have narrowed the gaps between such tracks during the last three to four decades. Usually, streaming to different tracks occurs later and common periods of education are longer even in other European *multi-track* "systems" (e. g. in the Dutch "system"). In 1967, S. B. Robinsohn published a critical evaluation of the German educational reform inertia and the non-preparedness "to modify the tripartite organization" of the school "system" (S. B. Robinsohn 1967, reprinted 1992, p. 87). For him, however, the essential question was, how the separation between general and vocational tracks could be overcome (see: op. cit., p. 91).

The traditional educational underpinnings of apprenticeships, hardly in line with the liberal philosophy of "equality of opportunity", deprive the majority of German youngsters *de facto*, not *de jure*, of access to higher levels of education and have generated over several generations a social and affective distance of Germans of humble social origins to education (see: R. Dahrendorf, 1965; S. Grimm, 1966; J. Oelkers, 2003).

The two lower tracks (Hauptschule, Realschule) of the traditional three-track "system" are the main tributaries of the "dual system". Its "forward defence" in lower secondary education is one of the major reasons for the ossification of the German education and training arrangement: a policy which rejects *equality of opportunity* and is based on the so-called principle of *Chancengerechtigkeit* (see: DIHK, 2001, S. 6), which can be understood as an updated version of the old Roman principle *suum cuique*.

The German multi-track "system" in effect is a *turbocharger* of the "dual system", as the impaired lower educational tracks leave apprenticeships as a large number of youngsters' only access road to the labour market with some prospects of "decent" work and salary levels. Lower tracks and apprenticeships may allure them in a triple sense:

(1) They seem to promise work opportunities, sometimes only with modest educational efforts. (2) Unlike other types of work preparation, apprenticeships offer monetary compensation independent from the parents' purse: a fact, which might be more tempting for candidates of humble social backgrounds than for their better-off peers. (3) Following different tracks in a multi-track "system" to different social destinations considerably homogenizes the *clientele* of each track, but keeps the particular track *clienteles* apart. Social learning, overarching the boundaries of each group, is not promoted, but hampered, and in some cases supports the development of snobbishness and unfriendly or even hostile attitudes towards outsiders. It is highly likely that different types of schools discriminate against different social clients, but exactly how this takes place is not sufficiently known, except for the case of ethnical differences (compare: M. Gomolla/F.-U. Radtke, 2007).

The German education "system" reduces the opportunities as well as the incentives for multi-dimensional learning including learning from other social experiences: an aspect which is not favourable for the development of empathy among social groups. "Group homogenization" and "social differentiation" have a potential to work hand in glove.

The Supply-Side Booster of Apprenticeships
(self-administration by the "social partners")

Apprenticeship design and supervisory bodies are usually *bodies of the economic system*, not of the education system and it should be remembered that apprenticeship systems are small nowadays, at least in economically advanced countries. Hence, supervision of such minority systems by bodies of the economic system is not surprising. But, it is astonishing that this is also the case in Germany, where a majority of young people in the recent past have undergone very heterogeneous apprenticeship training in a so-called secondary track, which has several disadvantages compared to other secondary provisions from an educational point of view. But, the design and supervisory bodies do not simply belong to the economic, but also to the particular German political "system", more specifically to the parts not based on voting.

The training system leads to tertiary levels only, when and insofar as the "customer" is willing to walk long and winding deviation routes. Thus, youngsters living in that educational sub-culture have to overcome more obstacles than youngsters in other European countries and apprenticeships and their educational underpinnings have dug out "educational grooves" with considerable retention effects. Parliamentary control (and public debate) of education and especially training, to which a large number of youngsters is subject, is deficient: a practice which secured the private sector a "privileged and ... very precisely targeted access to the most intelligent, performance-oriented and ambitious young people" (B. Lutz, 1995, S. 10)

The fact that the German apprenticeship "system" is numerically much larger in terms of the percentages of young age cohorts, than apprenticeship "systems" in other industrially advanced countries, is – on the basis of historically shaped mentalities and a certain cultural tradition – related to private sector self-administration of apprenticeships complemented by some trade union influence after the passing of the Vocational Training Act in 1969.

When governments and parliaments become involved in the design of apprenticeship standards, such regulations tend to include also other educational interests than only those of the companies and trade unions. Decision-making mechanisms which reflect a wider circle of constituents than just companies and trade unions tend to render apprenticeship curricula non-attractive, too burdensome or too remote from what potential training companies deem useful for their purposes and, therefore, are willing to finance. Maintaining a *mass* apprenticeship "system" *and* a democratic political system therefore are two goals not easily in harmony with each other and consequently one or the other must not be abolished, but reduced. In the German case, "people's sovereignty," or the electorate's political will, is "complemented" by *social (group) partnership* as the legitimizing principle and, thus, reduced. Otherwise the companies easily would stop training young people or reduce their training efforts. The German *mass* apprenticeship "system", therefore, defies substantial designs and/or controls by parliaments or ministries.

Temporary and easily-vanishing economic advantages (see: H. Kern/Ch. Sabel 1994; U. Weidenfeld, 2004) might be accompanied by more durable political disadvantages, which have to either be accepted in defence of the (assumed) economic advantages or to be rejected because of inherent political risks and fundamental democratic values: devaluation of parliaments in education and training matters; a concomitant watering down of A. Lincoln's famous principle "government of the people, by the people, for the people" (A. Lincoln, 1989, p. 536); "fraternization" between "economic" and "political classes" against the general electorate; alienation of the "political class" from the electorate; degradation of the electorate to the status of gullible voters etc.

It is a conspicuous fact, that the complicated German democratic "machinery" still is not sufficiently underpinned by a corresponding educative configuration, while many features of an education and training arrangement were preserved, which originated in pre-democratic times (see: S. B. Robinsohn 1967, reprinted 1992, p. 83; J. Oelkers 2003). There can be no doubt about the social and political relevance of the traditional three-track general education "system" (at present under reform pressure because of demographic and other reasons) and German apprenticeships since 40 – 70% of German youngsters have undergone apprenticeship training in recent decades. The joint effects of federalism and neo-corporatism have successfully blocked the democratization of the German education and training arrangement. Apprenticeship curricula are not subject to parliamentary or ministerial decision, and the vocational school curricula, are necessarily complementary appendices of apprenticeships. The "dual system" can only function (as a mass "system") when this is assured and the spokespersons of parliamentary parties usually offer such assurances. At present, the normative roles of German parliaments seem to be rather constrained in educational matters (see: G. Kutscha 1997, p. 672).

The Emergency Supply-Side Booster of Apprenticeships
(the partial elimination of the "market mechanism"
replaced by "political" and "ethical obligations")

The two permanent boosters are complemented by a third temporary one, which is switched on in times of economic downturns and/or in times of demographic peaks. The German private sector should offer training places according to social demand *under all conditions* and even when the free play of market forces does not suffice to do so: "When the government … transfers the task of practice-oriented vocational training to the employers, it is to be expected, that the social group of the employers fulfils this task according to their objective possibilities and in such a way, that, in principle, all youngsters looking for training have a chance to get a training place. This is also valid, when the free play of forces is not sufficient for the fulfilling of the assumed task." (Verdict of the Federal Supreme Court from December, 10th, 1980, quoted from H. Schmidt, 1996, S. 53)

Leaving training seekers without training offers could seriously endanger the apprenticeship system on the secondary level, which, if it were a pure and simple market system, would periodically "produce" a certain level of youth unemployment (youth without apprenticeship contracts). Government therefore – based on the Supreme Court's verdict – periodically wields "Damocles' sword" over the private sector's rights to implement and finance training, for instance, by threatening to introduce a levy-grant financing scheme. So far, governmental (announcement) policy has managed to squeeze more apprenticeship places from the companies' coffers than the market forces managed to do. Remaining "rests" where often trained in governmentally financed programs.

Nevertheless, although there are a high number of young people neither managing to get an apprenticeship contract nor entering a full-time vocational school, because of a variety of diverse reasons (40% of all training seekers), their foreseeable destiny on the labour market did not convince politicians that fundamental reforms are necessary. Often, there are solemn statements and declarations, but, so far, the required political actions and the related educational reforms still are in short supply. There is a wide gap between political rhetoric and political action, particularly when it comes to reform in German education and training.

The German apprenticeship system in the end of the 19th century was already in decline, when it was politically re-vitalized *before* Germany became a democratic nation. More than thirty years later, apprenticeships were tremendously invigorated, "generalized" and modernized by the Nazi regime, not least for disciplinary and martial purposes. Their distance to genuine educational tracks (the term "education" had a rather nasty ring for the fascists, who despised everything with civilizing effects) is much wider than the distance between general and vocational education tracks within genuine education systems. Nations with a longer democratic experience, especially the U.S., had a stronger desire to create configurations which also emphasized a certain tracking, but in the same time the needs of cohesion between citizens of the same polity consisting to a larger extent of immigrants of diverse cultural backgrounds: "A second explanation views the rise of vocational education as a natural outcome of expanding democratic societies bent on integration and socializing new citizens. In this "integrationist" argument, the major precipitating factors are unchecked immigration and an expanding clientele of secondary pupils (usually from working class background) due to the broadening of compulsory education laws." (A Benavot, 1983, p. 66) Even when different design and supervisory bodies are established *within* educational systems for general and vocational tracks, the gaps to be bridged are less wide than in the German case, which generates a wide gap between design and supervisory mechanisms of the education system and such mechanisms of the economic system, which reinforces the social tracking effect. Greinert's view is rather similar: The "independence of the vocational education system isolates it from the general education system" (2003, S. 85; see also: M. Baethge, 2001, S. 66). In the consequence, the contents and quality criteria of both systems are hardly compatible, as was already indicated in the sub-chapter about the "cultivation" implications of the "Beruf".

"Philosophies", contents, the different roles of scientific concepts versus economic practice-orientation, the "structured school system", different locations of the "bridgeheads to the labour market" (economic versus education system), the public-private dichotomy in ownership and the different design and supervisory bodies generate two sharply contrasting educational cultures in which different parts of the German population have followed for decades: Their divisive and unfavourable effects were documented by TIMSS and PISA. An educational culture divided into "high" and "low culture" comes into perspective which generates problems for parents of both cultures to accept their children walking down another educational path than what they deem "appropriate" or "promising" for their children's future (see: S. Grimm 1966, especially chapter V). Germans of humble social origins might be afraid of what their children have to cope with in Gymnasium and university, while better-off Germans are afraid of their children suffering from social decline, which seems to threaten them, once they fail to pass the "Abitur" and have to accept apprenticeships in the "dual system" (see: E. Middendorf 2002).

But, parents' choice is one thing, the other one is the supposedly very important discrimination effect of different types of schools, with their specific structures, functions, cultures, reputations, teachers, financial means etc. There is a need for empirical studies, how such effects come into existence and what their numerical dimensions are.

Lower social milieus nowadays have to cope with economically precarious situations, with diverse jobs and joblessness, with insecurity, which demands "a particular flexibility and virtuosity. ... In the final consequence the formation of a special mentality is of central importance to cope with insecurities and ruptures in the course of life." (Grundmann et al., S. 55) This is not favourable for stable long-term investment into the future, which the school requires.

Certainly, educational attitudes in Germany are changing, but there are some economic, political and cultural factors that keep such change in slow motion.

Since in the early seventies of the last century the "Sachverständigen-kommission *Costs and Financing of Vocational Education*" (members: F. Edding (President), H. Albach (Deputy President), Th. Dams, H. Gerfin, J. Münch) tried to identify systematically the costs of company-based training, the BIBB has examined costs and financing of apprenticeships usually in intervals of about ten years. The annual "Berufsbildungsbericht" ("Vocational Education Report"), mainly concerned with apprenticeships, which the Federal Government has to submit to parliament, normally juxtaposes "costs" and "benefits" (the result of apprentices' productive work in monetary terms). More specifically, these reports usually account for "gross costs" (Bruttokosten), benefits accruing by the productive work of apprentices, which, deducted from "gross costs", then result in "net costs" (Nettokosten).

While in much former political rhetoric "exploitation of apprentices" was assumed, because of phenomena in the history of German apprenticeship training like the so-called "breeding of apprentices" (Lehrlingszüchterei = recruiting and keeping apprentices not for training, but for profit-making purposes), the "Sachverständigenkommission" surprised the general public and many scientists as well, by giving evidence that German companies "invested" in apprenticeship training in aggregate, though not necessarily in all individual cases, and that they did not follow short-term cost-benefit calculations, but rather long-term considerations about their profitability. But, twenty years later, researchers still seem to be somewhat puzzled by their findings: "Why in the Federal Republic of Germany, though there are undeniable 'migratory dangers', companies invest systematically in marketable qualifications, is difficult to explain by the classic human capital theories." (U. Backes-Gellner, 1996, S. 307; *my translation – K. Sch.*) Already in 1969, W. D. Winterhager presented the results of his investigation on "Costs and Finances of Vocational Education" (W. D. Winterhager, 1969), and, the "founding father" of German educational economics, Friedrich Edding, summarized Winterhager's views in the preface of the publication as follows: "What in the practice of companies is done in training, contradicts the logic of the system …" (F. Edding, preface to W. Winterhager, 1969, S. 5; *my translation – K. Sch.*).

Since the early seventies scientists tried to identify the causes of the strange "investment" behaviour of German companies in the training field in more detail and a major breakthrough was achieved by D. Sadowski, who in 1980 showed that there are sound reasons for companies to offer training places, because – as he could give evidence – systematic training efforts can increase the companies' reputation on the labour market. In addition, training can be understood as an important and efficient tool of recruitment policy (Sadowski 1980). These findings were later taken into consideration in other studies undertaken by researchers of the BIBB and by various other scientists and practitioners. A well-known study in this field was the one presented by Cramer and Mueller in 1994. Their argument was: If one takes saved recruitment costs into consideration – saved because the company invested in training – then the cost – benefit – ratio becomes even more favourable. Consequently the annual "Vocational Education Report" from 2003, for instance (see p. 122), includes a juxtaposition of costs and benefits of apprenticeships in diagram form, which shows "total net costs" of Euro 7.344 per apprentice and considerable economic benefits of Euro 5.765 per apprentice because of saved recruitment costs, saved costs of work induction and saved costs for further education. But, even if one follows the report's arguments, a "minus" of Euro 1.579 remains. The report then argues that, if one would include "other non-quantifiable benefits" (named are: a lower mis-recruitment risk and lower fluctuation, avoidance of a deficit of specialized workers, long-term differentials between self-trained workers and externally hired workers, improvement of the company's image) the recruitment of workers/employees on the labour market would regularly be more expensive than the training of apprentices (Berufsbildungsbericht 2003, S. 121). Though this can be true in a number of cases, the argument seems to be rather daring as a generalization.

Apprenticeship training is not concerned with homogeneous occupational groups. Training in commercial and administrative fields is different from training in industrial manufacturing, different from occupations in the craft sector and different from training in the service sector and all these occupational fields are not homogeneous themselves. Therefore it is recommendable not to assume the same level of cost pressure between competitors, the same financing requirements, the same financing behaviour and the same financing motivation across economic sectors, occupations and firm sizes. While many companies train because there is no (significant) cost burden linked to apprenticeship training after the deduction of the monetary value of apprentices' productive work, while it includes other long-term benefits, in a considerable number of cases apprenticeship training clearly contributes to companies' profitability (see also: Mohrenweiser/Zwick, 2008). In other cases again, (especially bigger) companies might be in a position to neglect the net costs incurred by apprenticeship training while they appreciate their level of influence on educational matters, contents and structures and deem it worth considerable training investments. Such companies represent "the spearheads" of German training and they are financially capable, not to forget training as a cost factor, but to prioritize political considerations how to generate educational environments (or, at least to influence them in such a way), which they deem favourable for their main concerns.

This paper tried to open up a new route in the understanding of German companies' behaviour concerning training. It gives evidence that the exclusion of political reasons in cost-benefit-ratios must produce biased results. Cost-benefit-ratios focusing exclusively on economic rationales must produce a purely economic explanation – and this does not look realistic according to the line of arguments presented above. Profitability is certainly essential for companies, but it does not exclude other goals and strategies and the German political context offers companies and their "Verbände" particular opportunities to influence educational matters. Purely economic approaches necessarily make efforts to find more and more economic benefits, including such benefits, which often seem to escape numerical determination, if they occur at all. Although they can occur here and there, in a number of cases they seem to be far-fetched. The exclusion of political reasons from the cost-benefit-ratios lends analyses on German companies' "investment" in apprenticeships a detached character – detached from the full mix of reasons, especially as well-known private sector representatives do not fail to hint on considerations relevant in the sense of this paper (L. Späth, 2003).

In general, in the scientific literature, macro-economic analyses tend to treat training as an "investment", while micro-economic ones are more divided, but partly opt for "costs". R. Von Bardeleben, U.

Beicht and K. Feher (authors of the BIBB) have argued that the "investment" viewpoint is doubtful insofar as German apprentices are free to leave their training company once the apprenticeship period is over. As they actually leave their employers in numerous cases (in large numbers even before their apprenticeships are completed), a "pure" investment perspective is questionable.

But, the strange training behaviour of German companies becomes less strange, if cost-benefit considerations are not exclusively based on economic reasons, but include political elements as well. In addition, there is a need to differentiate especially between economic sectors and occupations.

Then, motives of what is often called "investment" could be subsumed under three or four major headings like the following:

- (a) *Short-term profit-making reasons*; training costs occur, but are lower than direct economic benefits of training, hence improve the short-term profitability of companies;
- (b) *Long-term profit-making reasons*; training costs are higher than mere training benefits, but have some long-term advantages and desirable outcomes beyond the "narrow" training perspective. As many large employers offer "more" and more specific training contents during apprenticeships than what is prescribed by training ordinances and as many apprentices want to stay with such training providers after their apprenticeship periods are over (they usually offer the best salaries, the best employment prospects and the best career opportunities), training can be seen as an investment in order to bring apprentices' skills and competences up to a sufficient level for the companies' needs, but also improving the image of the company on the labour market, improving its reputation as a "socially responsible employer" etc.;
- (c) *Risk minimization*: Apprenticeships in large companies might include an insurance fee against mis-recruitment of risky "external" candidates;
- (d) *"Maintenance tax" for a political privilege in a parliamentary democracy*: The "maintenance tax" might be paid by larger companies only in order to convince politicians from different political strands and also the general public about the usefulness of the apprenticeship configuration (see: BWP, Heft 4/2002, S. 6 – 13) and to support the maintenance of its general education tributaries.

Of course, the mix of considerations is rather varied and economic and political rationales underlying apprenticeships might not be the same in differently sized companies, in companies operating in different economic branches and also might not be the same in companies, chambers and other private sector organizations. Concerning the mix of relevant considerations within the private sector as a whole, more empirical investigations would be required than what is presently available. We still do not know too much about such reasons in a complex system of de-centralized decision-making shielded against insights from the general public. The more training and training financing is removed from the companies' decision-making centres, the more they are vulnerable by other influences, which makes companies often suspicious vis-à-vis "überbetriebliche Finanzierung", payroll taxes etc. As long as training and training financing remain largely under the companies' discretionary power, it is likely to be perceived as "investment" and portrayed as such for the wider public, but the perception could change into a "tax burden", once financial decision-making concerning apprenticeships is removed from companies' decision-making processes. Even chamber-controlled financing schemes might have their drawbacks and weaken the already weakened traditional affiliation of German companies to training.

Meanwhile the financing of training has undergone considerable changes and company-based financing of training is complemented by public means. Since many years the federal as well as the regional governments support apprenticeship training by billions of Euro, they also finance particular programs for youngsters without training contracts and they subsidize group training centres under the supervision of the chambers. The EU is also involved in the financing of training. In other words, European and German citizens pay, but they neither have a chance to (directly or indirectly) determine the number of training places, nor the contents of training (see for instance: J. Roitsch, 2004, S. 870).

The article tried to identify the mixed reasons why German companies "invest" in apprenticeships: besides economic reasons also political ones were identified. But, a question remains: do German companies "invest" in apprenticeships, shoulder a "cost" burden or are such assumptions based on statistical and accounting illusions? From an economic circuit perspective it could be argued, that it is likely that customers pay for apprenticeships, because "cost factors" (however evaluated in economic theory: costs, investments, taxes etc.) can be partially or totally pushed ("überwälzt") onto customers' shoulders – either national or international, which would mean customers have to pay, but citizens have no say in such an arrangement. Concerning such questions, we face the same problems as before: theoretical considerations are difficult to corroborate by empirical studies in a non-public system.

Creative Destruction, Vested Interests and Reform Perspectives

Creative Destruction and Special Interest Collusion:
The Need for New Factor Combinations

Schumpeter's and Olson's Approaches:
Technological, Economic and Social Innovations

Besides being essential for each individual citizen' life, non-formal family education, formal education in schools, colleges and universities and training in companies and vocational schools or training institutes are more or less powerful energy providers to various social sectors. One of the main receivers of their provision is the economy. The purposes of education and training, therefore, are comprehensive and they should not be reduced to economic functions to the detriment of their other roles. But, while their functions are comprehensive and should not be narrowly understood or defined, the energy supply of education and training to the economy deserves attention. Education and training influence the level on which economic factors can be combined and are an integral part of such combinations, in the knowledge-based society a decisive one. More sophisticated production concepts and products usually require not only higher levels of educational achievement and attainment, but also a turning away from the elements of particular forms of socialization for particular social groups, which may have survived from earlier historical periods. Hence, the general educational level plays a role, if there are wide educational gaps between different population groups or not and if these groups are socialized in more or less traditional conditions, based on social origins, or in democratic forms, which have a capacity to equalize socialization processes – to some extent.

It was due to J. A. Schumpeter's (1883 – 1950) scientific breakthrough that for the first time in history theories about old and new factor combinations could be formulated and about the processes, fundamental in capitalism, which he described as "creative destruction" as well as about the so-called "long waves" of economic development. Already in his book from 1911 "Theory of economic development" statements about the replacement of old factor combinations by new ones can be found: "To produce means to combine things and forces available for us (in unserem Bereiche). ... : it can happen, but it is not essential, that the new combinations are pushed through by the same persons who dominate the production process ... in those traditional, old combinations" (J. A. Schumpeter, 1994, S. 100/101). In 1942 he diagnosed that the process of economic growth "incessantly revolutionizes the economic structure *from within*, incessantly destroying the old one, incessantly creating a new one. This process of Creative Destruction is the essential fact about capitalism." (J.A. Schumpeter, 1993, S. 137/138; quoted from W. Easterly, 2002, p. 177/178)

He even explained in some detail the character of the essential kind of competition he had in mind. His explanation is a "heavy weight" for the understanding of global competition, including the variations in the cultural and institutional endowments of different countries. Schumpeter explains various types of competition and claims that conventional forms are "not important, but the competition of the new commodity, the new technology, the new provision source, the new organization type (...) – that kind of competition, which commands a decisive cost or quality advantage and which hits the existing companies not at their profit and production limits, but in their proper life marrow." (J. A. Schumpeter, 1993, S. 140)

When Schumpeter wrote down his thoughts about "creative destruction" and old and new factor combinations, rigid types of work organization, based on taylorist concepts of the division of labour were dominant and technological and economic innovations seemed to cause social change in a "one way traffic". Economic and technological changes induce structural changes in society, not so much the other way round, social changes improve societies' capacities to perform economic and technological tasks. In that period of time there still was a wide gap between imparting manual skills on the one hand and education for other work tasks (and social destinations) on the other. Under such conditions concepts of democratic education and socialization and what was thought to be economically effective, were worlds apart. Meanwhile the importance of generally high cognitive levels and democratic requirements alike make it possible and necessary to overcome those gaps. Overcoming them became not only desirable because of democratic reasons, but a necessity because of the competitive advantages they entail. Advanced factor combinations

include workforces on generally high levels of educational achievement and attainment, avoiding looming gaps of the educational levels
of different social groups and also leaving older socialization forms
behind, based on social origins. This makes new ways possible how
economic factors can be combined, which could not be perceived in
Schumpeter's lifetime.

His description of "new factor combinations" – in the presently
prevailing terminology he probably would have written about "innovations" – echoes the spirit of the time, despite the persisting importance of his thought. The prevalence of technological, organizational
and other economic innovations clearly resonate in the terms "the
new technology" and "the new organization type". But, the last three
to four decades have given evidence that other "innovations" are possible too (which does not mean technological or organizational innovations would become irrelevant), particularly "social innovations"
based on a new type of mass education and democratic and "generalized" socialization, which implies a far-reaching turning away from
traditional forms. This type of "new factor combinations" has been
extremely successful on the world markets. Some societies might not
find it easy to change from older modes of delivery to the required
new modes, especially when they are linked to mixed ownership of
education and training (like in the German case) because one or the
other owner might feel threatened by the required changes.

Persons, groups or countries linked to old factor combinations are
subject to decline, while persons, groups or countries linked to new
and advanced ones are bound to rise, hence, there are winners and
losers in creative destruction. This is the point of entry for Mancur
Olson's theory. It is obvious that persons or groups working with old
factor combinations may have a vested interest, which can become an
incentive to oppose creative destruction and the replacement of older,
less efficient factor combinations by newer and more advanced ones.
Olson therefore formulates an essential implication of his theory that
such social forces opposed to change, are inclined to engage in various
defensive activities and in coalitions. "Distributional coalitions", in
his theory, "slow down a society's capacity to adopt new technologies
and to reallocate resources in response to changing conditions, and
thereby reduce the rate of economic growth." (M. Olson, 1982, p.
65) But "coalitions" and "special-interest groups" are not necessarily

confined to strictly "distributional activities", but may include a much wider circle of aspects, including political ones, as Olson himself has pointed out: "In the case of those distributional coalitions that seek their objectives by political action, the reason for exclusion is that there will be more to distribute to each member of the coalition if it is a minimum winning coalition." (op. cit, p. 66) And: "Imagine a country or historical period in which some subset of the population, such as the nobility or the oligarchy, dominates the political system. This subset has an incentive to choose public policies that distribute more of the social output to its own members. Except in the case where the aristocracy or oligarchy would increase its security if new members (for example, powerful rivals) were added, it will be exclusive: every unnecessary entrant into the favoured subset reduces what is left for the rest. The relevance of this argument is evident from the exclusiveness of governing nobilities throughout history." (M. Olson, 1982, p. 67)

In these examples politics is used as a tool of distributional activities concerning financial resources, goods and services. But, if "distributional coalitions", "special-interest collusion", "cartels" turn from distributional aims concerned with the "social output" to politics as their main target, then "coalitions" "distribute" political power according to certain patterns of collusion and according to the "strength" of the individual coalition members' position in that coalition (which does not exclude an "arranged" distribution of the social output). Under certain political circumstances such coalitions may show an otherwise and elsewhere unlikely capacity to survive. Unfortunately, this is relevant in the German case.

The Particular Nature of the German "Distributional Coalition"

It was attempted in the initial sections to explain the complexity of German *interlocking politics* as a result of two sources of political legitimacy: one generated by voters' ballots, the other one by "social partner" agreement. A couple of political fields are "cut out" from the general political process, based on voting, and are subject to bargaining processes between the "social partners", probably the most important among the "cut-out"-areas is training, which requires a "stabilization" of general education structures, so that sufficient participant numbers of an at least sufficient capability are channelled to the training area. This, in turn, requires a very particular public-private-partnership between the public and the private owners of the general education + training configuration. A re-structuring of general education, especially a transformation of the multi-track into a one-track configuration would put the "dual system" into jeopardy, hence political competences and privileges of the private sector and the "Verbände", which would also touch upon the timberwork of the German party-"Verbände"-democracy.

While general education in principle is subject to voters' decision, the "dual system" in its core (the supply of training places and the design of training standards), is not. In addition, the Vocational Training Act from 1969, as already shown, did not change the training system, but codified the apprenticeship system as a mono-integrated system of the private sector, as it was, with a minor change concerning the inclusion of the trade unions into some training decision-making processes. In other words: from Germany's social plutonic rock a pre-democratic structure did not cease to tower into the present German society and still causes the non-modernity of German modernity in various dimensions. In the reduced party-"Verbände"-democracy two contrasting and opposing principles are effective – a fact with consequences: they can only be linked to each other by turning the voters ballots "innocuous".

On the way from the ballot box to the parliaments voters' decisions were and are interpreted by deputies belonging to parliamentary parties (like in other countries too), but, in such a way in Germany, that it seems desirable to leave the education and training structures as they traditionally were and still are, notwithstanding how conditions have changed, however modern and advanced educational requirements altered and whatever international education and training developments might be concerned with. Declaring the "dual system" to be "the world's best training system" or a "location advantage" (Standortvorteil) for Germany, or the self-aggrandizing baptism of Germany as the "world champion in training" are convenient input factors for such policies. The party-"Verbände"-democracy "freezes" an arrangement, which therefore cannot keep pace with international requirements and loses, as time goes by, its ability to supply sufficient energies to the German economy.

The power balance and the power sharing between government, the private sector and their "Verbände" remain untouched and this allows partial educational reforms only, namely the optimization of the sub-systems, while control over the sub-systems essentially remains unchanged. There are also other effects: The stabilization of the party-"Verbände" democracy reduces the sovereignty of the electorate, turns "democracy" in the education and training field into a vacuous concept, leaves (parts of) the population unaware of the importance of education, and thus contributes to educational complacency. It also has undesirable consequences in the field of political worldviews.

There is something "unsound" in the German condition, as long as the parties and the "Verbände" regard voters as a potentially disturbing or damaging factor concerning the governance of the education and training sector.

Education and Training Policies and their
Effects in the Economic "System"

The interdependency between education and economics and economics and education has been seen, in many cases, as a one-sided dependent relation in Germany: with education as the sub-system completely dependent from the development of the economic system and unable to dynamize the economy by better inputs on higher levels of educational attainment and achievement. Consequently, more sustained educational efforts of more citizens were discouraged and the high-low-divide of the German educational culture maintained. The request "Send your child for a longer period of time to better schools" (Schick dein Kind länger auf bessere Schulen) was called "a disastrous educational policy postulate". It was criticized that longer education was preferred "contrary to all international experiences on the labour market" and it was also claimed, that "suitability, talents and performance potential and interests of youth would not have been taken into consideration". R. Dahrendorf's position concerning "Education is the Right of Citizens" was called "detached from training needs" (for all quotations, see: Ministerium, 1995, S. 3). Private sector representatives had similar misgivings about more young people reaching higher attainment levels: "Today, much too many students travel in inadequate educational departments and trains. Today every third of an age cohort strives for a university degree, tomorrow already forty percent shall do so. There are cities – e.s g. Bonn, Göttingen, Heidelberg, Marburg, Tübingen -, in which the share of Gymnasium students among all students is much higher than 50%. With 1.823.000 the number of university students in the winter semester 1992/1993 has reached a new record level. In our educational policy debates much too rarely the question is raised, if the desired educational target – Abitur and possibly university degree – does not exceed the abilities and forces of many young people, if one does not paralyze truly existing talents, and especially if one does not prevent them from making successful experiences and sends them with the terrible burden to the labour market to be a failure, a drop-out." (W. Schlaffke, 1994. S. 18/ 19) The "Fachkraft" was declared to be the "key figure of the competitive 'Made in Germany' " (W. Schlaffke, 1994, S. 20) and the myth of those "talented for the crafts" (handwerklich Begabte) was revitalized (op. cit., S. 21) – a late salute to Kerschensteiner. The terms utilized are typical for employees trained on a sub-academic level and they are certainly needed, but German educational policies did not get the dimensions right.

Many such statements could be quoted which all had the tendency to argue against higher participation rates in general education, especially on more advanced levels (Gymnasium and university), while vocational tracks, and especially the "dual system", were favoured. The much too low German participation rates in tertiary education can partly be traced back to such messages, which were sent on an almost daily basis and did not fail to impress the public. Therefore, analyzing the German PISA results, harangues by private- and public-sector officials decrying "academization" and "over-qualification" should not be overlooked.

Besides an inadequate care for the energy supply of a dynamic and therefore always changing economic "system", there is also the question, if other roles of general education were appropriately taken into account, especially general education's role to take care of a well-rounded educational "equipment" of society and the instilling of democratic ideals into young Germans.

Despite such policies the proverbial catholic worker's girl from rural areas sometimes succeeded nevertheless to embark on an educational journey her mother perhaps had not even dreamt of. But, the German educational expansion, by far, did not reach other countries' proportions. A comparison with other European and with East Asian countries would show, that in exactly that period of time, when the German educational constellation became more ossified than ever, Japan, for example, embarked on an "incredible" educational expansion (see: M. B. Jansen, 2000, pp. 748/749). Meanwhile, Australia, Canada, Finland, France, (South) Korea, Sweden and other countries have chosen similar roads and some may travel on them in perhaps even higher gears and similar things can be said from China and India – but their numbers are incomparably bigger.

A blocked or strangled training and education arrangement necessarily has unfavourable effects on other social "systems" as well. Education and training as a still life cannot contribute to economic dynamism, even when the configuration, once upon a time, had been the envy of the world.

The "Distributional Coalition of All Social Forces" and Freedom of Speech

The prescription and imposition of an "orthodox" or "correct view" does not only happen under despotic rule. It can also happen – in more mild-mannered forms, with less draconian, nevertheless serious consequences – in parliamentary democracies, when a "distributional coalition" becomes that dominant that it must not any more fear to be challenged by one or several powerful rivals. The risk that such a development may occur is especially threatening in countries like Germany where the voters' influence on politics – because of the understandable political precaution after World War II – was kept extremely indirect, while some sectors were *de facto* even kept beyond voters' reach, because of the inclusion of "Verbände" into the political power structure. Such circumstances invite the emergence of privileged party-"Verbände"-relations, which easily sideline the electorate in "ingenious" ways. A "distributional coalition" under such conditions can become "almighty" either by defeating the remaining rival(s) or by integrating them into the coalition. In Germany the "distributional coalition" concerning power in the education and training field managed to integrate the final remaining critics of the "dual system", especially in the trade unions in 1969. While the early conservative German governments after World War II were one-sided in their "Verbände" predilections, the CDU/CSU/SPD-government (the "big coalition"-government) from 1966 to 1969 integrated the trade unions into the German party-"Verbände"-democracy, which came of age by the passing of the Vocational Training Act in 1969.

After the trade unions had been included into the "distributional coalition", and the coalition had proved its stability for several years, from around the mid-seventies, the "dual system" ideology was in full flight and the unexportable object of adoration became even an export article, though landings on foreign soil were neither smooth "element-wise", nor wholesale. In the paper he read in 1989 during the conference of the Committee for Educational Economics of the "Verein für Sozialpolitik" in Trier, D. Timmermann said: "Regardless of controversial assessments of the system structures and the system performances, meanwhile, during the last 15 years, a social fundamental consensus of all social groups emerged ("darüber hergestellt") that the Dual System of vocational training is not only irreplaceable as a system, but, in the contrary, the best of all vocational education systems. In international comparisons of different vocational education systems the advantages of the Dual System (...), which meanwhile was promoted to the factor No. 1 of the location quality of the Federal Republic of Germany, are especially to be seen in ..." (a number of characteristics and performances are enumerated) (D. Timmermann, 1989, S. 4; see also: W.-D. Greinert, 1995, S. 2; BMBF (ed.), Second International Congress on Technical and Vocational Education – Documents presented by the delegation of the Federal Republic of Germany, Bonn 1999).

Declaring the "dual system" irreplaceable amounts to power and competence presumption, because such statements touch upon parliamentary and governmental prerogatives in a democracy, when the affairs under consideration are of general social and political importance, which is certainly the case with a training arrangement of the size of the "dual system". Federal parliament still is not involved in the design of training standards and the related decision-making and the executive departments of government rubber-stamp the bargaining results of the "Verbände" about training standards into law. The voter is sidelined. Such procedures cry out for additional fortifications, which were erected by damaging freedom of speech in the education and training sector. K. Heimann explained the relevant mechanism in a rare statement in 1992: "The dual system in practice has been canonized, and everybody who dared to make a scratch on it, practically was somebody, who had, so to say, to be excluded." (K. Heimann, 1993, S. 20)

Several questions could be raised:
- From what?
- By whom?
- Which social areas were particularly affected?
- Cui bono?

"Canonization" and "exclusion" sound like a strange mixture of religious and social/political expressions, but their meaning in everyday life is neither holy, nor mixed. It is not unknown what they stand for in mundane affairs and in social practice. Hans Albert explained in his "Treatise on Critical Reason" (Traktat über kritische Vernunft): "The *purpose of the installation of dogmas* is not so much the solution of problems of recognition or of morale, but the rejection of inadequate, which means, of such solutions, which are regarded by the authorities concerned as dangerous. It opposes the free deliberation of alternative solutions and shall serve the fixing (establishment) of problem solutions accepted by the authorities and therewith in the same time assuring the existence of the institutions linked to the creed system by the elimination of persons of a different faith, that means, of such individuals which do not submit to the authorities concerned." (H. Albert, 1991, S. 116)

Heimann's restraint and unassuming statement is of the utmost importance for the understanding of the "dual system's" persisting existence and size, its multi-track underpinnings and for the fact that Germany "overslept" the educational expansion in other parts of the world. Actually international educational expansion was *not* overslept, but incomprehensive and therefore inadequate reforms were the outcomes of vested interests and of the given balance of power in the German political system, which generated a kind of a religious cult, turning the "dual system" into the golden calf, exactly in that period of time, when it had become more doubtful than ever. When freedom of speech is damaged in a certain sector, the sector's further development is at stake, which in a dynamic world not agreeing to grind to a standstill in consideration of German internal mechanisms necessarily invites failure. When differentiated arguments are needed, the imposition of something canonized by an unofficial, but effective *de facto* punishment (exclusion) of dissenters depreciates the cons, elevates the pros to undeservedly strong position and perhaps even to the status of infallibility, which is not only not democratic but also ill-advised.

While the dichotomy of "canonization" and "exclusion" knows only two states of affairs, human frailty in social life knows many more, including fallibility, hypocrisy and opportunism. Imposing a creed necessarily spoils the atmosphere, which is detrimental to the open and frank discussion of required strategies, changes and reforms. German society meanwhile has to pay the price for the "canonization" of the "dual system", which is – together with the multi-track general education – one of the major causes of social rigidity and mass unemployment, not going away soon, despite recent favourable trends.

The petrification of a social sub-arrangement in a dynamic world damages the functioning of other "systems" as well. When the education and training "system", one of the major energy suppliers to the economy, is bound to move within a given mould, it is only a matter of time till the consequences are to be felt in economic affairs. This is the case in a divided education and training configuration, not easily to be changed by the electorate, when the knowledge-based society arrives. What always has been a political problem, but for a long time was accompanied by economic dynamism, now turns into a twin problem concerning both, the health of the German democracy and German economic performance as well. So far, German exports are still remarkably strong and the picture is not completely gloomy, but more penalties are likely to arrive, if fundamental structural reforms are further delayed.

Not only, but also therefore, the "party-"Verbände"-democracy" needs to be further developed into the parliamentary democracy of the civil society. "The attempt to develop a democratic conception of the political good – … – does not offer, it should be stressed, a panacea for all injustices, evils and dangers (…). But it does lay down good grounds for the defence of a public dialogue and decision-making process about matters of general concern, and suggests institutional paths for its development. My argument is not that 'democracy' is the answer to all questions – far from it – but that, when adequately clarified and explicated, democracy can be seen to lay down a programme of change in and through which pressing, substantive issues will receive a better opportunity for deliberation, debate and resolution than they would under alternative regimes." (D. Held, 1996, p. 298)

The "big difficulty" in conceiving government of persons over persons seems to touch upon a double governmental capacity: at first government must be able to control the governed, while then the government must be forced to control itself. "The dependency from the people is without doubt the best instrument, to keep a tight rein on government." (The Federalist, quoted from Chr. v. Krockow, 1971, S. 104) How this could be achieved in the modern "mass democracy" seems to be an unsolved problem, not only in Germany, but, more so, when democratic principles and corporatist principles exist side by side to the detriment of both, the citizens and the democratic principles, while the political parties seem to have become rather independent from the voters (see: G. Dahrendorf, 2002, S. 702). They seem to be prepared to grab power with decreasing and perhaps with the tiniest of voter turnouts in a period of time when political parties seem to have changed into "party machines" or "power machines", linked to a variety of sources of power besides the citizens. Essentially the democratic combination of power and people is not completely replaced, but pushed to the background by an equally well-known one, the combination of power and money (see: G. Dahrendorf, 2002, S. 702; see also: C. Crouch, 2008, pp. 4-7).

The existing double linkage between education and training and politics on the one hand and education and training and the economy on the other, needs to be understood, when fundamental education and training reforms are envisaged in Germany. What has been internationally regarded as an important cause of German economic dynamism in the past seems to be outdated nowadays. But, when structural education and training reforms are uno actu political reforms, they are difficult to achieve, because they touch upon the existing balance of power. When it is true that the knowledge-based society requires another education and training configuration than earlier economic stages, the German democratic deficit cannot be justified any more by a plus of economic dynamism compared to other varieties of capitalism and democracy. Lacking dynamism has many sources, but there are reasons to assume that the German arrangement of education and training is among the culprits.

The developments and reforms of the sixties of the last century – the expansion of general education, the Vocational Training Act from 1969 – remained piecemeal reforms, because they did not achieve a comprehensive reform of the whole education and training system, but remained confined to an optimization of both partial systems – higher general education on the one hand and vocational education and training on the other.

Concluding Remarks

Solving structural education problems in Germany looks similar to dissolving the "Gordian Knot". The persisting situation is such, that once a structural string in education or training would be pulled, the balance of power between the private and the public sector, the balance between the federal government and regional governments, the balance between employers' associations and trade unions, the power of various teachers' organizations and different school forms etc. would be affected; hence, not to move seems to be "politically wise". German educational inertia is not simply caused by the penetrating power of tradition and educational conservatism, but by a surprising finding: the German configuration of politics, economics, education and training does not signal a "functional differentiation of partial social systems" in Luhmann's vein, but a lack of such differentiation and a partial fusion of "partial systems of society" (see also statements by J. Berger, 2003, S. 210). When the "political system" is regarded as the provider of "binding decisions" for the society, it should not remain unnoticed that curriculum decisions on the secondary level for the training of about 40% of German youngsters (a short while ago of 55 to 70%) were "produced" by "Verbände", neither by what is understood as "the political system" in Luhmann's terms nor in a common sense understanding.

Still, a dis-solution of the "Gordian Knot" is not impossible, but difficult to achieve. On the other hand, there are penalties on not achieving, some of them of a heavy calibre.

Germany has strayed from her path as a front-runner in mass education and training in former times. Contrary to the older generations, Germany's youngsters are not as well educated in an internationally comparative perspective than their forebears and they reach less high attainment levels than their competitors according to official sources. "Many other countries in the foreseeable future have a better starting position. They have rearranged their education and training system ("Ausbildungssystem") in time for the requirements of the knowledge-based economy, the young generation there probably is better trained for the demands of the economy – and their up- and -coming generation is more numerous." (see: BMBF, 2003; especially the section on "Die verschleppte Dynamik im deutschen Bildungssystem").

If we take the OECD's PISA studies as a yardstick, we do know with some measure of certainty, that streaming children at the tender age of ten to the existing different tracks is neither a good thing for the children nor for Germany as a whole. These tracks do not simply represent curriculum diversification or performance levels, but include heavy social tracking. Politicians carry responsibility for not putting "the system question" (J. Oelkers, 2003) on the agenda and for delaying structural educational reform, which contributes to mistrust in political parties and politics in general, to Germany's fading economic dynamism, during the last twenty to thirty years, and also to growing social woes. Such effects are reminders of *several* debates and missed reform opportunities during the last century.

Luckily, there was not only party strife and haggling after PISA, but also a couple of thoughtful statements from politicians of different political strands, from chamber representatives, scientists and from journalists as well (see for instance: M. Spiewak, 2002; L. Spaeth, 2003; J. Hogeforster, 2003; J. Oelkers, 2003; U. Weidenfeld, 2004; Chr. Füller/M. Böhmann, 2004; Chr. Füller, 2008). But, it is well known that structural changes in education are hard to achieve under German circumstances, because they touch upon entrenched interests of a strong coalition of privileged groups, including the political parties and the powerful "Verbände". If regional parliaments, competent in educational affairs, with their diverse majorities, worldviews, traditions, problems, and affiliations with the "Verbände", muster sufficient energies to push *unanimously* through new and *compatible* concepts in favour of the education of high percentages of the German population *on high attainment levels*, seems to be more than questionable, at present. The "demographic factor" though might push through some educational reforms – e. g. the reduction of the number of educational tracks – at least in some states of the German federation.

Interlocking politics might produce another political deadlock, thus preserving the existing structures, while merely pedagogical reforms are likely to be less effective than what is needed. Educational structures do not only produce individual educational performance or aggregates of individual achievement, but also contribute to social integration or segregation, aspects relevant not only in social life, but also in the world of work, contributing to comparative economic efficiency or inefficiency. Old-fashioned and outdated educational arrangements are certainly not the only sources of unfavourable phenomena, but they have a capacity to contribute to ineffective habits, authoritarian and dictatorial manners and management styles and they certainly don't improve and enhance economic and other performances. It is ironic that German companies have tried to copy foreign production concepts (just-in-time, lean production, flat hierarchies, profit centres, group or team work, total quality management, continuous improvement processes etc.), while the modernization of underlying processes of education, training and socialization was continuously refused.

Modern and democratic concepts can comprehensively contribute to economic and other performances only, if and when based on corresponding educational processes. They also would promote inclusiveness, trust, fairness, equality, good or not so good vertical and horizontal cooperation patterns, open promotion opportunities, hence, energy and enthusiasm. If the discussion of "achievement" after PISA does not include the afore-mentioned viewpoints, achievement still can be enhanced by highly expensive programs within the old and rigid structures. But, such policies would leave the other relevant aspects more or less untouched, like socialization patterns based on social origins. According to A. Overesch Finland's PISA success is underpinned by "a rather homogeneous social structure", which the population seems to cherish. "Education is evaluated as an instrument to reach this goal." (A. Overesch, 2008; see also: A. Overesch, 2007)

Avoiding *any* structural change in the education and training arrangement would be a risky strategy from educational (low average achievement, wide achievement spread), social (high unemployment rates, stabilization of an underclass), economic and financial (costs of unemployment, enormous governmental budget deficits on all levels, international competition), as well as political points of view (abstention, apathy, anti-democratic effects). Therefore, safer options should be preferred. Germany has been an "early bird" in implementing mass education and training – in pre-democratic times and forms – and has caught the economic "worm" (other "worms" she caught are under-researched). Because of the ossification of her educational structures, the country risks to fall internationally behind, particularly in tertiary education enrolments, which does not bode well for her future economic competitiveness. There are a couple of reform alternatives, but fundamental and comprehensive educational reforms so far still seem to be beyond the horizon.

Summary

The German combination of apprenticeships (complemented by courses in group training centres) and vocational school education, known under the label "dual system", is the outcome of historical evolution and intentional policy. While the historical character of German apprenticeships was often emphasized in the past and is well known therefore, purposive designs and planning were not absent in their modern development. Revitalized after a period of decline, apprenticeships played an increasing role in German manpower policies at the turn of the 20th century in a situation of "state emergency". They were complemented by "further education schools" (the forerunners of the "vocational schools") and, thus, contours emerged of what became much later known as the "dual system" (only after 1964).

These attempts were part of conservative and liberal policies (these terms explain less than one might be inclined to think) to stem the rising tide of political challenges of the semi-feudal/semi-democratic Prussian/German state. Governmental defence strategies consisted in the illegalization and oppression of opponents, in the stabilization of the "Mittelstand", linked to the reinvigorated development of the chambers, authoritarian youth policies, in the development of various social insurance systems, and in the pursuit of coalition policies with all social and political forces willing to maintain the "status quo". An element of such policies was the transfer of certain "rights of authority" to private sector organizations, particularly to the chambers of the crafts. In the same time, while the promotion of vocational education and training (not: technical education and training) in the frame of promotional policies for the "Mittelstand" had a stabilizing but illiberal character, it supported German industrial dynamism – a complex mixture of strategies and outcomes sometimes described by historians of different creeds as "conservative" or "reactionary dynamism" or "modernism". The effects of the chosen "policy mix" tragically alienated Germans of humble social origins from the then German state, thus, effects were rather profound. Vocational education and training, especially after industries adopted the craft-based apprenticeship model in ever increasing numbers, contributed to Germany's rising industrial power on the world markets before 1914.

The "Dual System" was revitalized, de-centralized and partly "de-governmentalized" after World War II in a situation when the Allied Powers tried to re-establish democracy after the defeat of Nazism. Because of the need to prevent the resurgence of dictatorial policies a wide diffusion of political power was designed while the voters were largely seen as unreliable by German and foreign politicians and other observers. Popular sovereignty was cautiously introduced though not in all sectors. A not very transparent "democratic machinery" and a complicated governmental structure were designed including "social organizations", which left the electorate with a bare minimum of possibilities to determine governments and policies. This is the background, why government is less a "monolithic" power and political actor in Germany than in many other industrially advanced countries. It is more a relation between public and private sectors and it is this pattern of "interlocking politics" which was firmly established in the training sector, but not, as observers might be inclined to assume, the public, but the private sector taking the lead.

The fact is explained, why Germany's apprenticeship system has an astonishingly large intake of youngsters, compared to apprenticeship systems in nearly all the other economically advanced societies. Only smaller companies train mainly because of economic reasons, while bigger companies train because of a variety of economic, non-economic and political reasons. They defend a rare privilege in parliamentary democracies, namely the private sector privilege to design and implement mass-relevant training standards and to shape the skills, competences, attitudes and mentalities of a large number of young people, in fact, for many years a majority of the country's young generation.

Influencing people's minds and personalities does not stop at the borders of the training sector and has repercussions in the structure of the general education system as well. The apprenticeship system contributes to making Germany's tertiary education sector much smaller than comparable sectors in other economically advanced countries. While in the past this was more or less unanimously seen as a German competitive advantage, present mood seems to be more undecided and contradictory. Many experts, at present, not least from the OECD, perceive Germany's comparative low student enrolment in the tertiary education sector as threatening future German economic performance in a period of increasingly knowledge-based processes.

The paper offers some historical and political explanations, a criticism of neoclassical and "common sense" models in comparative vocational education research, and an inspection of structures, institutions and "boosters" of the "dual system's" performance. The question, why German companies and private sector institutions "participate" not only in training but also in *training design,* targets a very clear behavioural difference between German entrepreneurs and the entrepreneurs of many other countries. It is largely a question concerning the social forces which have a decisive say in design, supervision and implementation of training.

Non-investment in training is a piece of circumstantial evidence that entrepreneurs might deem their level of influence on training too low and therefore decide not to invest in the production of vocational skills and competences. Hence, the behavioural differences between German and many other international entrepreneurs are not simply caused by cultural differences (though they play an important role), but by peculiarities of German political history. These peculiarities have brought forth a peculiar German governmental concept, which includes a "transfer" of training into the sphere of entrepreneurs' responsibilities and their "Verbände". It goes without saying that such outcomes of history are not easily to be transferred and implanted into other contexts. German entrepreneurs' "quasi" training monopoly in the "dual system" has become extended to an asymmetric duopoly in 1969 which grants trade unions a minor role. In order to make use of the internationally rather unusual situation and of the rights and power chances linked to it, German entrepreneurs are willing to maintain the established division of labour between government, "private interest government" and the trade unions, which they still deem favourable for their main concerns. Hence, they are willing "to invest" in training. Seen from this angle, it becomes clear, that German entrepreneurs' training attitude is neither simply fuelled by "humanist" or "social" motives nor simply an expression of "German culture" (which it is too), but a shrewd utilization of the rare opportunity – by international standards – to condition their workforce's mentality and competences on which their business success depends.

Training is not free of charge, but, by "investing" in training, they prevent other social groups and factors to have a bigger say in the German education and training arrangement, especially government, parliament, ministerial bureaucrats and society at large. If the term "dual system" is justified, it is more because of the peculiar interplay between company-based training and market forces on the one hand and regulation by the "Verbände" (entrepreneurs' associations and trade unions) according to the "Beruf" (vocation or calling) concept, not because of the company – vocational school – duality, which is not a fundamental mechanism in the German training "system".

This perspective is hardly to be gained, if the analysis concentrates on vocational education and training as such. The factors causing German entrepreneurs to train can only be adequately perceived, when training is placed into the wider framework of the historical construct of the German state-society-concept. By examining the motivations behind German training a rather multifaceted bundle of reasons is identified, which defies simple explanations, like "tradition", "habits", "social responsibility", "investment", "image improvement", "economic cost-benefit-ratios" and the like. It is certainly not based upon faulty mathematics. Instead, a particular, nation-specific mix of political, economic and other reasons, based upon particular cultural underpinnings, is relevant for the exceptional training engagement of German companies. The fact that "dual systems" exist in Austria, Germany and Switzerland gives evidence of the importance of the cultural fundaments of "dual systems". Nevertheless, the intricacies of the three "systems" differ and their politico-cultural environments as well. The paper tries only to explain the German case.

The penultimate chapter is focused on J. A. Schumpeter's and M. Olson's theories of economic growth, hence on economic factor combinations and on social coalitions promoting new factor combinations or defending old ones because of vested interests. Such combinations and social coalitions are important in the field of human resources development in the transition from advanced factor combinations based on secondary mass schooling and training to more advanced factor combinations based on tertiary mass education. The governance systems of education and training can become an obstacle for the implementation of newer factor combinations, which in turn slows down economic growth and therefore has rising levels of unemployment in train. In this case far-reaching reforms might become necessary which may include interlinked political and educational reforms.

Bibliography

Abel, H., Das Berufsproblem im gewerblichen Ausbildungs- und Schulwesen Deutschlands (BRD), Braunschweig 1963.

Abelshauser, W., Kulturkampf – Der deutsche Weg in die Neue Wirtschaft und die amerikanische Herausforderung, Berlin 2003.

Abelshauser, W., Wirtschaftliche Wechsellagen, Wirtschaftsordnung und Staat: Die deutschen Erfahrungen. In: D. Grimm (Hrsg.), Staatsaufgaben, Frankfurt/M. 1996, S. 199 – 232.

Abraham, K., Der Betrieb als Erziehungsfaktor – Die funktionale Erziehung durch den modernen wirtschaftlichen Betrieb, Köln 1953.

Albert, H., Die Wissenschaft und die Fehlbarkeit der Vernunft, Tübingen 1982.

Albert, H., Marktsoziologie und Entscheidungslogik, Tübingen 1998.

Albert, H., Traktat über kritische Vernunft, Tübingen 1991 (5. verbesserte und erweiterte Auflage).

Altmann, R., Berufsausbildung und Selbstverwaltung. Zur Struktur der betrieblichen Lehre. In: DIHT (Hrsg.), Die Verantwortung des Unternehmers in der Selbstverwaltung, Frankfurt am Main 1961.

Amonn, O., Die Gesellschaftsordnung und ihre natürlichen Grundlagen. Entwurf einer Social-Anthropologie zum Gebrauch für alle Gebildeten, die sich mit sozialen Fragen befassen, Jena 1900 (3. Auflage).

Archer, M. S., Social Origins of Educational Systems, London – Beverly Hills 1979.

Arnim, H. H. v., Staat ohne Diener, München 1993.

Backes-Gellner, U., Betriebliche Bildungs- und Wettbewerbsstrategien im deutsch-britischen Vergleich, München und Mering 1996.

Baethge, M., Ausbildung und Herrschaft – Unternehmerinteressen in der Bildungspolitik, Frankfurt am Main 1971 (4. unveränderte Auflage).

Baethge, M., Beruf – Ende oder Transformation eines erfolgreichen Ausbildungskonzepts? In: Th. Kurtz (Hg.), Aspekte des Berufs in der Moderne, Opladen 2001, S. 39 – 68.

Baethge, M., Berufsprinzip und duale Ausbildung: Vom Erfolgsgaranten zum Bremsklotz der Entwicklung? In: W. Wittwer (Hrsg.), Von der Meisterschaft zur Bildungswanderschaft, Bielefeld 1996, S. 109 – 124.

Baethge, M./Baethge-Kinsky, V., Jenseits von Beruf und Beruflichkeit? – Neue Formen von Arbeitsorganisation und Beschäftigung und ihre Bedeutung für eine zentrale Kategorie gesellschaftlicher Integration. In: Mitteilungen aus der Arbeitsmarkt- und Berufsforschung (MittAB), 31. Jg., 1998, Heft 3: Wandel der Organisationsbedingungen von Arbeit, S. 461 – 487.

Baethge, M./H. Solga, M. Wieck, Berufsbildung im Umbruch – Signale eines überfälligen Aufbruchs, Berlin 2007.

Bardeleben, R. v./Beicht, U., "Investitionen in die Zukunft" – eine bildungsökonomische Betrachtung der Berufsausbildung aus betrieblicher Sicht. In: Zeitschrift für Berufs- und Wirtschaftspädagogik (ZBW), Heft 12/ 1996, S. 22 – 41.

Bardeleben, R. von/U. Beicht/ K. Feher, Betriebliche Kosten und Nutzen der Ausbildung, Bielefeld 1995.

Bas, D., Cost-effectiveness of training in developing countries. In: International Labour Review, Vol. 127, 1988, No. 3, pp. 355 – 369.

Bas, D., On-the-job training in Africa. In: International Labour Review, Vol. 128, 1989, No. 4, pp. 485 – 496.

Bau, H./Th. Stahl (Hrsg.), Entwicklung einer Kooperationskultur im dualen System der beruflichen Ausbildung, Bielefeld 2002.

Becker, W./W. Lauterbach (Hrsg.), Bildung als Privileg – Erklärungen und Befunde zu den Ursachen der Bildungsungleichheit, Wiesbaden, 2007 (2. aktualisierte Auflage).

Benavot, A., The Rise and Decline of Vocational Education. In: Sociology of Education, 1983, Vol. 56 (April): pp. 63 – 76.

Benner, H./H. Schmidt, Kapitel 3.1.1. "Historische Entwicklung" (S. 1 – 12). In: Cramer/Schmidt/Wittwer (Hrsg.), Ausbilder-Handbuch – Aufgaben, Strategien und Zuständigkeiten für Verantwortliche in der Aus- und Weiterbildung, Köln 1994.

Benoehr, S., Das faschistische Verfassungsrecht Italiens aus der Sicht von Gerhard Leibholz, Baden-Baden 1999.

Berger, J., Neuerliche Anfragen an die Theorie der funktionalen Differenzierung. In: H.-J. Giegel/U. Schimmank (Hg.), Beobachter der Moderne – Beiträge zu Niklas Luhmanns "Die Gesellschaft der Gesellschaft", Frankfurt am Main 2003, S. 207 – 230.

Berger, K./G. Walden, Zur Praxis der Kooperation zwischen Schule und Betrieb – Ansätze zur Typisierung von Kooperationsaktivitäten und –verständnissen. In: G. Pätzold/G. Walden (Hg.), Lernorte im dualen System der Berufsbildung, Bielefeld 1995, S. 409 – 430.

Beyme, K. v., Das politische System der Bundesrepublik Deutschland – Eine Einführung, Opladen/Wiesbaden 1999 (9. Auflage).

BIBB (ed.): H. Sauter/H. Schmidt, Training Standards in Germany – The development of new vocational education and training (VET) standards (state-recognized training occupations), Bonn 2002.

BIBB (Hg.), Mechatroniker/Mechatronikerin: ein neuer staatlich anerkannter Ausbildungsberuf, Bonn 2000.

BMBF – Bundesministerium für Bildung und Forschung (Ed.), Second International Congress on Technical and Vocational Education – Documents presented by the delegation of the Federal Republic of Germany, Bonn 1999.

BMBF – Bundesministerium für Bildung und Forschung (Hg.), Zur technologischen Leistungsfähigkeit Deutschlands, Bonn 2003.

BMBF (Hrsg.), Berufsbildungsbericht 2003, Bonn 2003.

Bowland, D. L., Co-Ordination of Training Systems – Some Basic Issues (Training Policies – Discussion Paper No. 25), Geneva 1988.

Breuer, St., Ordnungen der Ungleichheit – die deutsche Rechte im Widerstreit ihrer Ideen, 1871 – 1945, Darmstadt 2001.

Bruchhäuser, H.-P., Bildungspolitik und Bildungstheorie – Das berufspädagogische Erbe des 19. Jahrhunderts. In: Zeitschrift für Berufs- und Wirtschaftspädagogik (ZBW), 96. Band, Heft 4/2000, S. 495 – 511.

Bureau International du Travail (ed.): C. Maldonado et al., L'économie informelle en Afrique francophone – Structure, dynamiques et politiques, Geneve 2001.

Burrow, J. W., Die Krise der Vernunft – Europäisches Denken 1848 – 1914, Muenchen 2003.

Conze, W., Beruf. In: O. Brunner/W. Conze/R. Koselleck (Hrsg.), Geschichtliche Grundbegriffe. Historisches Lexikon zur politisch-sozialen Sprache in Deutschland, Stuttgart 1994 (4. Auflage).

Coy, M. W. (ed.), Apprenticeship – From Theory to Method and Back Again, New York 1989.

Cramer, G., Wie würde sich eine Ausbildungsabgabe auf ausbildende Grossbetriebe auswirken? – Eine persönliche Bewertung. In: Berufsbildung, 51. Jg., Dezember 1997, Nr. 48, S. 18 – 19.

Cramer, G./Kh. Mueller, Nutzen der betrieblichen Berufsausbildung. Beiträge zur Gesellschafts- und Bildungspolitik Nr. 195, Köln 1994.

Crouch, C., Postdemokratie. In: Neue Gesellschaft/ Frankfurter Hefte, No. 4/2008.

Dahrendorf, R., Bildung ist Buergerrecht – Plädoyer für eine aktive Bildungspolitik, Hamburg 1965.

Dahrendorf, R., Neue Rechte als Kritik etablierter Parteien. In: Merkur , Heft 8, 56. Jg., August 2002, S. 700 – 704.

Deißinger, Th., Beruflichkeit als "organisierendes Prinzip" der deutschen Berufsausbildung, Mering 1998.

Deißinger, Th., Das Konzept der "Qualifizierungsstile" als kategoriale Basis idealtypischer Ordnungsschemata zur Charakterisierung und Unterscheidung von "Berufsbildungssystemen". In: Zeitschrift für Berufs- und Wirtschaftspädagogik, 91. Bd., 1994, Heft 4, S. 367 – 387.

Deißinger, Th., Zum Problem der historisch-kulturellen Bedingtheit von

Berufsbildungssystemen – Gibt es eine "Vorbildfunktion" des deutschen Dualen Systems im europäischen Kontext? In: Th. Deissinger (Hrsg.), Berufliche Bildung zwischen nationaler Tradition und globaler Entwicklung, Baden-Baden 2001.

Deutscher Industrie- und Handelskammertag (Hrsg.), Duale Berufsausbildung, Berlin 2003.

DIHK – Deutscher Industrie- und Handelskammertag (Hrsg.), Bildungsstandort Deutschland – Leistungspotentiale erschließen, Berlin – Bonn 2001.

Dostal, W./F. Stooss/L. Troll, Beruf – Auflösungstendenzen und erneute Konsolidierung. In: Mitteilungen aus der Arbeitsmarkt- und Berufsforschung (MittAB), 31. Jg., 1998, Heft 3, S. 438 – 460.

Easterly, W., The Elusive Quest for Growth – Economists' Adventures and Misadventures in the Tropics, Cambridge (Massachusetts) (MIT Press).

Ebert, R., Zur Entstehung der Kategorie Facharbeiter als Problem der Erziehungswissenschaft, Bielefeld 1984.

Edding, F., Vorwort. In: W. D. Winterhager, Kosten und Finanzierung der beruflichen Bildung, Stuttgart 1969, S. 5 – 6.

EIU (The Economist Intelligence Unit), Knowledge workers revealed – New challenges for Asia, Hong Kong 1998.

Englert, L. (Hrsg.), Georg Kerschensteiner – Eduard Spranger, Briefwechsel 1912 – 1931, München 1966.

Euler, D., Modernisierung des dualen Systems – Problembereiche, Reformvorschläge, Konsens- und Dissenslinien, Bonn 1998.

Faulstich, P. (Hg.), Die Bildungspolitik des Deutschen Gewerkschaftsbundes 1949 – 1979, Stuttgart 1980.

Friedeburg, L. v., Bildungsreform in Deutschland – Geschichte und gesellschaftlicher Widerspruch, Frankfurt am Main 1989.

Füller, Chr., Schlaue Kinder, schlechte Schulen, München 2008.

Füller, Chr./M. Böhmann, PISA 2003: Nach der Grundschule wird verlernt – Error Hauptschule. In: Die Tageszeitung, 4./5. 12. 2004, S. 3.

Galuske, M., Zur Pädagogik Eduard Sprangers. In: Zeitschrift für Berufs- und Wirtschaftspädagogik (ZBW, Beiheft 9: Historische Berufsbildungsforschung), 1992, S. 27 – 42.

Georg, W./A. Kunze, Sozialgeschichte der Berufserziehung – Eine Einführung, München 1981.

Gomolla, M., F.-O. Radtke, Institutionelle Diskriminierung – Die Herstellung ethnischer Differenz in der Schule, Wiesbaden 2007 (2. durchgesehene und erweiterte Auflage).

Green, A. (with A. Sakamoto), Models of High Skills in National Competition Strategies. In: Ph. Brown, A. Green, H. Lauder (eds), High Skills – Globalization, Competitiveness, and Skill Formation, Oxford – New York 2001, pp. 56 – 160.

Greinert, W.-D., Berufsqualifizierung und dritte Industrielle Revolution, Baden-Baden 1999.

Greinert, W.-D., Das duale System der Berufsausbildung in der Bundesrepublik Deutschland – Struktur und Funktion, Eschborn 1992 (hrsg. von der Deutschen Gesellschaft für Technische Zusammenarbeit (GTZ)).

Greinert, W.-D., Das duale System der Berufsausbildung in der Bundesrepublik Deutschland – Struktur und Funktion, Stuttgart 1995 (2. verbesserte Auflage), Holland und Josenhans.

Greinert, W.-D., Die große Lähmung – oder: wie demontiert man "das beste Ausbildungssystem der Welt"?. In: Berufsbildung, Juni 1995, 49. Jg., Heft 33, S. 2.

Greinert, W.-D., Geschichte der Berufsausbildung in Deutschland. In: R. Arnold/A. Lipsmeier (Hrsg.), Handbuch der Berufsbildung, Opladen 1995, S. 409 – 417.

Greinert, W.-D., Organisationsmodelle und Lernkonzepte in der beruflichen Bildung, Baden-Baden 2000.

Greinert, W.-D., Realistische Bildung in Deutschland – Ihre Geschichte und ihre aktuelle Bedeutung, Baltmannsweiler 2003.

Greinert, W.-D., Regelungsmuster der beruflichen Bildung: Tradition – Markt – Buerokratie. In: Berufsbildung in Wissenschaft und Praxis, Heft 5/ 1995, S. 31 – 35.

Greinert, W.-D., Schule als Instrument sozialer Kontrolle und Objekt privater Interessen: Der Beitrag der Berufsschule zur politischen Erziehung der Unterschichten, Hannover 1975.

Greinert, W.-D., Über den notwendigen Umbau des dualen Systems der Berufsausbildung – Vom "ordnungspolitischen Instrument" des `19. zum "praxisbezogenen Qualifikationsmodell" des 21. Jahrhunderts. In: Berufsbildung, Januar 1996, 50. Jg., Heft 37, S. 3 – 7.

Grimm, S., Die Bildungsabstinenz der Arbeiter, München 1966.

Grundmann, M. et al., Bildung als Privileg und Fluch – zum Zusammenhang von lebensweltlichen und institutionalisierten Bildungsprozessen. In: R. Becker/W. Lauterbach (Hrsg.), Bildung als Privileg – Erklärungen und Befunde zu den Ursachen der Bildungsungleichheit, Wiesbaden 2007 (2., aktualisierte Auflage), S. 43 – 70.

Hagedorn, J. R., Ausbildungsabgabe vernichtet Lehrstellen. In: Berufsbildung, 51. Jg., Dezember 1997, Nr. 48, S. 8 – 9.

Hall, P.A./D. W. Soskice, Varieties of Capitalism. The Institutional Foundations of Comparative Advantage, Oxford University Press 2001.

Hansjosten, H., Lohnt sich die betriebliche Ausbildung? – Eine Studie am Beispiel der DaimlerChrysler AG, München und Mering 2000.

Harney, K./P. Storz, Strukturwandel beruflicher Bildung. In: D. K. Mueller

(Hrsg.), Pädagogik – Erziehungswissenschaft – Bildung, Köln – Weimar – Wien 1994, S. 353 – 381.

Haxby, P., Apprenticeship in the United Kingdom: from ITBs to YTS. (complemented by D. Parkes, Recent Developments in the UK Training Scene). In: European Journal of Education, Vol. 24, No. 2, pp. 167 – 181.

Hegelheimer, A., Finanzierung der beruflichen Ausbildung – Financing of Vocational Training, Mannheim 1986 (bilingual edition: German – English).

Heidenreich, M., Die duale Berufsausbildung zwischen industrieller Prägung und wissensgesellschaftlichen Herausforderungen. In: Zeitschrift für Soziologie, Jg. 27, Heft 5, Oktober 1998, S. 321 – 340.

Heimann, K., Contribution during the panel discussion on "Is the dual system threatened? Quality and attractivity of dual training". In: BIBB (Hg.), Metall/Elektro – Konzepte und Probleme nach fünf Jahren Neuordnung und zwei Jahren Vereinigung, Nürnberg 1993.

Heinz, W. R., Berufliche Bildung zwischen Wertewandel und betrieblicher Modernisierung. In: S. Liesering/K. Schober/M. Tessaring (Hg.),. Die Zukunft der dualen Berufsausbildung, Nürnberg 1994, S. 110 – 123.

Held, D., Models of Democracy, Stanford/California 1996 (2nd edition).

Hennis, W., Aufgabe und Grenze der Parteien. In: W. Hennis, Die missverstandene Demokratie, Freiburg i. Brsg. 1973, S. 135 – 143.

Hennis, W., Der "Parteienstaat" des Grundgesetzes – Eine gelungene Erfindung. In: W. Hennis, Auf dem Wege in den Parteienstaat, Stuttgart 1998, S. 107 – 135.

Hennis, W., Ein einig Volk von Zuschauern: Wozu ist das Wahlrecht da? In: W. Hennis, Auf dem Wege in den Parteienstaat, Stuttgart 1998, S. 136 – 141.

Hesse, H. A., Berufe im Wandel – Ein Beitrag zum Problem der Professionalisierung, Stuttgart 1968.

Hilbert, J. et al., Berufsbildungspolitik: Geschichte – Organisation – Neuordnung, Opladen 1990.

Hofstadter, R., Social Darwinism in American Thought, Boston 1955 (revised edition).

Hüfner, K., Bildungswesen mangelhaft – BRD-Bildungspolitik im OECD-Länderexamen, Frankfurt am Main 1973.

Hylla, E., Die Schule der Demokratie – Ein Aufriss des Bildungswesens der Vereinigten Staaten, Langensalza, Berlin und Leipzig 1928.

Interview mit J. Hogeforster: "Den Schulen Freiheit geben" – Der Chef der Hamburger Handwerkskammer, Jürgen Hogeforster, über Nachwuchssorgen, neue Formen des Lernens und das Versagen des gegliederten Schulsystems. In: Die Zeit, Nr. 41/2003, 02. 10. 2003.

Ito, M., Qualitätsmanagement in Japan – ein kurzer Abriss seiner Entwicklung. In: M. Esser/K. Kobayashi (Hg.), Kaishain – Personalmanagement in Japan, Göttingen 1994, S. 114 – 123.

Jansen, M. B., The Making of Modern Japan, Cambridge (Massachusetts) – London 2000.

Katzenstein, P. J., Policy and Politics in West Germany – The Growth of a Semisovereign State, Philadelphia 1987 (Temple University Press).

Kaufmann, F.-X., Varianten des Wohlfahrtsstaats – Der deutsche Sozialstaat im internationalen Vergleich, Frankfurt am Main 2003.

Keiichi, Y., Der Trend zu tertiären Bildungsabschlüssen und die Berufskarriere von Universitätsabsolventen. In: H. Demes/W. Georg (Hg.), Gelernte Karriere – Bildung und Berufsverlauf in Japan, München 1994, S. 319 – 349.

Keim, W., Erziehung unter der Nazi-Diktatur, Bd. 1: Antidemokratische Potentiale, Machtantritt und Machtdurchsetzung, Darmstadt 1995.

Keim, W., Erziehung unter der Nazi-Diktatur, Bd. 2: Kriegsvorbereitung, Krieg und Holocaust, Darmstadt 1997.

Kern, H., Der Betrieb als Erziehungsinstitution. In: Kw. Stratmann/W. Bartel (Hrsg.), Berufspädagogik – Ansätze zu ihrer Grundlegung und Differenzierung, Köln 1975, S. 153 – 163 (reprinted from the original version from 1971).

Kern, H./Ch. Sabel, Verblasste Tugenden – Zur Krise des deutschen Produktionsmodells. In: Soziale Welt, Sonderband 9: Umbrüche gesellschaftlicher Arbeit (hrsg. von N. Beckenbach/W. v. Treeck), Göttingen 1994, S. 605 – 624.

Kerr, C., The Balkanization of Labor Markets. In: E. W. Bakke et al. (eds), Labor Mobility and Economic Opportunity, Cambridge/Mass. 1954.

Kerschensteiner, G., Der Weg zum Pflichtbewusstsein. In: G. Kerschensteiner, Deutsche Schulerziehung in Krieg und Frieden, Leipzig – Berlin 1916, S. 34 – 61.

Kerschensteiner, G., Der Weg zur Staatsgesinnung. In: G. Kerschensteiner, Deutsche Schulerziehung in Krieg und Frieden, Leipzig – Berlin 1916, S. 62 – 93.

Kerschensteiner, G., Die Probleme der Nationalen Einheitsschule. In: G. Kerschensteiner, Deutsche Schulerziehung in Krieg und Frieden, Leipzig – Berlin 1916, S. 126 – 242.

Kerschensteiner, G., Die Schule als Kulturmacht. In: G. Kerschensteiner, Deutsche Schulerziehung in Krieg und Frieden, Leipzig – Berlin 1916, S. 94 – 125.

Kerschensteiner, G., Georg Kerschensteiner – Selbstdarstellung (1926). In: G. Wehle (Hg.), Georg Kerschensteiner, Texte zum pädagogischen Begriff der Arbeit und zur Arbeitsschule – Ausgewählte pädagogische Texte, Bd. II, Paderborn 1982 (2. Auflage).

Kerschensteiner, G., Über das eine und einzige Ziel der Erziehung in Krieg und Frieden. In: G. Kerschensteiner, Deutsche Schulerziehung in Krieg und Frieden, Leipzig – Berlin 1916, S. 1 – 33.

Kerschensteiner, M., Georg Kerschensteiner – Der Lebensweg eines Schulreformers, Muenchen – Berlin 1939.

Kliebard, H.M., Schooled to Work: Vocationalism and the American Curriculum, 1876 – 1946, New York and London 1999.

Ko, Yoo-Jin, Better and Longer Term Advice on Industry Skill Needs (Comments). In: The Korea Institute for Industrial Economics and Trade (KIET)/Maeil Business Newspaper (eds), International Symposium on Demand-Led Human Resources Development: A Business-Led Industrial Approach, Seoul October 30th, 2003.

Koenen, E., Selbstbegrenzung des Staates in der Berufsbildung. In: V. Ronge, Am Staat vorbei – Politik der Selbstregulierung von Kapital und Arbeit, Frankfurt am Main – New York 1980, S. 83 – 124.

Kolnai, A., War against the West, London 1938.

Konietzka, D., Ausbildung und Beruf – Die Geburtsjahrgänge 1919 – 1961 auf dem Weg von der Schule ins Erwerbsleben, Opladen/Wiesbaden 1999.

Kottmann, M./E. Staudt, Die Lücke zwischen gewerblicher und akademischer Ausbildung blockiert Innovationen! In: Berufsbildung in Wissenschaft und Praxis, Heft 3/2001, S. 41 – 45.

Kraul, M., Das deutsche Gymnasium 1780 – 1980, Frankfurt am Main 1984.

Krell, G., Vergemeinschaftende Personalpolitik: Normative Personallehren, Werksgemeinschaft, NS-Betriebsgemeinschaft, Betriebliche Partnerschaft, Japan, Unternehmenskultur, München und Mering 1994.

Krockow, Chr. v., Soziale Kontrolle und autoritäre Gewalt, München 1971.

Krockow, Chr. von, Warnung vor Preußen, Berlin 1999.

Kuratorium der deutschen Wirtschaft für Berufsbildung (Hg.), Berufsausbildung auf dem Prüfstand – Fachtagung 1993 der gewerblich-technischen Ausbildungsleiter, Bonn 1994.

Kutscha, G., Berufsbildungspolitik. In: D. Kahsnitz/G. Ropohl/A. Schmid (Hrsg.), Handbuch zur Arbeitslehre, München – Wien 1997, S. 649 – 686.

Lauglo, J., Vocational Training: Analysis of Policy and Modes. Case Studies of Sweden, Germany and Japan. In: S.-Y. Lim/K. Schaack (eds): J. Lauglo, Education, Training and Contexts – Studies and Essays, Frankfurt am Main 2003, pp. 207 – 275.

Leidner, M., Wenn der Geselle den Lehrling ausbildet – Eine Analyse der pädagogischen Sinndeutungen und subjektiven Theorien nebenberuflicher Ausbilder im Bauhandwerk, Frankfurt am Main 2001.

Lenhardt, G., Kapitel 13: Bildung. In: H. Joas (Hg.), Lehrbuch der Soziologie, Frankfurt am Main 2001, S. 311 – 334.

Lincoln, A., Address at Gettysburg, Pennsylvania. In: A. Lincoln, Speeches and Writings, 1859 – 1865, New York 1989.

Linton, D. S., "Who has the youth, has the future" – The campaign to save young workers in imperial Germany, Cambridge 2002.

Lutz, B., Es geht um die Zukunft qualifizierter Industriearbeit. In: Müntefering, F., (Hrsg.), Jugend – Beruf – Zukunft, Marburg 1995, S. 8 – 22.

Mayer, Chr., Entstehung und Stellung des Berufs im Berufsbildungssystem. In: Zeitschrift für Pädagogik, 40. Beiheft: Beruf und Berufsbildung – Situation, Reformperspektiven, Gestaltungsmöglichkeiten, Weinheim und Basel 1999, S. 35 – 60.

Mayer, K.-U., Arbeit und Wissen: Die Zukunft von Bildung und Beruf. In: J. Kocka/C. Offe (Hrsg.), Geschichte und Zukunft der Arbeit, Frankfurt/M. – New York 2000, S. 383 – 409.

Meyer, R., Qualifizierung für moderne Beruflichkeit, Münster 2000.

Middendorf, E., Sozialgruppenspezifische Beteiligung an höherer Bildung – Ein Phänomen mit Geschichte (Teil 1). In: Das Hochschulwesen, 50. Jg., Heft 4/2002, S. 140 – 144.

Middendorf, E., Sozialgruppenspezifische Beteiligung an höherer Bildung – Ein Phänomen mit Geschichte (Teil 2). In: Das Hochschulwesen, 50. Jg., Heft 5/2002, S. 186 – 194.

Miegel, M., Die deformierte Gesellschaft – Wie die Deutschen die Wirklichkeit verdrängen, Berlin – München 2002 (3. Auflage).

Ministerium für Wissenschaft und Forschung Baden-Württemberg (Hg.), Berufsakademie Baden-Württemberg – Ausbildungskonzept, Berufsakademiegesetz, Ausbildungs- und Prüfungsordnung, Gleichstellungsverfügung, Gremienverordnung, Geschäftsordnung der Gremien, Stuttgart 1995 (*quoted as*: Ministerium).

Ministry of Education, Science, Sports and Culture, Japan (ed.), Education in Japan 2000, Tokyo 1999.

Ministry of Foreign Affairs/Danida, Vocational Education and Training, Copenhagen 1994.

Mohrenweiser, J./Th. Zwick, Why Do Firms Train Apprentices? The Net Cost Puzzle Reconsidered. ZEW Discussion Paper No. 08-019 (Zentrum für Europäische Wirtschaftsforschung, 2008)

Mommsen, H. (with M. Grieger), Das Volkswagenwerk und seine Arbeiter im Dritten Reich (Kapitel 4.3 "Eisen erzieht": Die Ausbildung einer deutschen Facharbeiterelite im VW-Vorwerk Braunschweig, S. 227 – 249), Düsseldorf 1997 (3. Auflage).

Mommsen, W. J., Die 'deutsche Idee der Freiheit'. In: W. J. Mommsen, Bürgerliche Kultur und politische Ordnung – Künstler, Schriftsteller und Intellektuelle in der deutschen Geschichte 1830 – 1933, Frankfurt am Main 2000, S. 133 – 157.

Moura Castro, C. de/T. Alfthan, International Differences in Vocational Training. Reprinted in: K. Schaack/R. Tippelt (eds): C. de Moura Castro, Vocational Training at the Turn of the Century, Frankfurt/M. 2000.

Müller, Kh., Kosten und Nutzen der Berufsausbildung. In: Kuratorium der deutschen Wirtschaft für Berufsbildung (Hg.), Berufsausbildung auf dem Prüfstand – Fachtagung der gewerblich-technischen Ausbildungsleiter, Bonn 1994, S. 29 – 38.

Münch, J., Umlagefinanzierung – ein bildungspolitisches Problem. In: Berufsbildung, 51. Jg., Dezember 1997, Nr. 48, S. 3 – 7.

Muth, W., Berufsausbildung in der Weimarer Republik, Wiesbaden 1985.

North, D. C., Institutions, Institutional Change and Economic Performance, Cambridge 1990.

OECD (ed.), Redefining Tertiary Education, Paris 1998.

Oelkers, J., Der Matthaeus-Effekt. In: Süddeutsche Zeitung, 04. 06. 2003.

Offe, C., Berufsbildungsreform – Eine Fallstudie über Reformpolitik, Frankfurt am Main 1975.

Olson, M., The Rise and Decline of Nations – Economic Growth, Stagflation, and Social Rigidities, New Haven and London 1982.

Overesch, A., Wie die Schulpolitik ihre Probleme (nicht) löst, Münster 2007

Overesch, A., Das finnische Erfolgsgeheimnis (Interview). In: Die Zeit, 20.03.2008, Nr. 13.

Papcke, S., Diesseits oder jenseits der Freiheit? Die Deutschen suchen ihren Standort zwischen Ost und West. In: W. Weidenfeld (Hg.), Nachdenken über Deutschland – Materialien zur politischen Kultur der Deutschen Frage, Köln 1985, S. 100 – 121.

Pätzold, G. (Hrsg.), Berufsschuldidaktik in Geschichte und Gegenwart – Richtlinien, Konzeptionen, Reformen, Bochum 1994.

Peisert, H., Soziale Lage und Bildungschancen in Deutschland, München 1967.

Pempel, T. J., Policy and Politics in Japan – Creative Conservatism, Philadelphia 1982 (Temple University Press).

Plessner, H., Die verspätete Nation – Über die politische Verführbarkeit bürgerlichen Geistes. In: H. Plessner, Gesammelte Schriften VI: Die verspätete Nation, Frankfurt/M. 1982, S. 7 – 223.

Plessner, H., Grenzen der Gemeinschaft – Eine Kritik des sozialen Radikalismus, Frankfurt am Main 2002.

Polanyi, K., The Economy as Instituted Process. In: M. Granovetter/R. Swedberg (ed.), The Sociology of Economic Life, Boulder/Colorado 2001, pp. 31 -50.

Preuß, H., Das deutsche Volk und die Politik, Jena 1916.

Pries, L., "Arbeitsmarkt" oder "erwerbsbezogene Institutionen"? Theoretische Überlegungen zu einer Erwerbssoziologie. In: Kölner Zeitschrift für Soziologie und Sozialpsychologie, 50. Jg., März 1998, Heft 1, S. 159 – 175.

Rabinbach, A., Human Motor – Energy, Fatigue, and the Origins of Modernity, Berkeley and Los Angeles 1992.

Raddatz, R., Beruf. In: GTZ (Hrsg.), Fachglossar: Deutsche Berufsbildungsbegriffe, Eschborn 1999.

Rahn, S., Der Doppelcharakter des Berufs – Beobachtung einer erziehungs- und sozialwissenschaftlichen Debatte. In: Zeitschrift für Pädagogik, 40. Beiheft: Beruf und Berufsbildung – Situation, Reformperspektiven, Gestaltungsmöglichkeiten, Weinheim und Basel 1999, S. 85 – 100.

Rauner, F./G. Spöttl, Der Kfz-Mechatroniker – Vom Neuling zum Experten, Bielefeld 2002.

Reble, A., Geschichte der Pädagogik – Dokumentationsband, 1999b (4. edition, first published: 1971).

Reble, A., Geschichte der Pädagogik, 1999a (19. revised edition, first published: 1951).

Reinhold, M., Neue Ansätze in der industriellen Berufsausbildung: Der Modellversuch "Geschäfts- und arbeitsprozessbezogene, dual-kooperative Ausbildung (GAB)". In: BWP, Heft 6/2002, S. 44 – 48.

Ringer, F. K., The Decline of the German Mandarins – The German Academic Community, 1980 – 1933, Hanover and London 1990.

Robinsohn, S./J. C. Kuhlmann, Two decades of non-reform in West-German education. In: D. Phillips (ed.), Education in Germany – Tradition and reform in historical context, London and New York 1995, S. 15 – 35; reprint from 1967.

Rohlen, Th., Differences that Make a Difference: Explaining Japan's Success. In: W. K. Cummings/Ph. G. Altbach (eds), The Challenge of Eastern Asian Education – Implications for America, Albany 1997, pp. 223 – 248.

Roitsch, J., Lehrstück Ausbildungsplatzabgabe. In: Blätter für deutsche und internationale Politik, 49. Jahrgang, Heft 7/2004, S. 862 – S. 870.

Rosenberg, H., Die Berufsvorbereitung des Industriearbeiters und ihre Bedeutung im Kampf um die Arbeitsfreude, Köln 1930.

Rosenzweig, B., Erziehung zur Demokratie? – Amerikanische Besatzungs- und Schulreformpolitik in Deutschland und Japan, Stuttgart 1998.

Rösner, E., Hauptschule am Ende – Ein Nachruf, Münster 2007.

Sachverständigenkommission *Kosten und Finanzierung der beruflichen Bildung,* Kosten und Finanzierung der außerschulischen beruflichen Bildung, Bielefeld 1974.

Sadowski, D., Berufliche Bildung und betriebliches Bildungsbudget, Stuttgart 1980.

Sadowski, D., Zur Theorie unternehmensfinanzierter Investitionen in die Berufsbildung. In: W. Clement (Hg.), Konzept und Kritik des Humankapitalansatzes, Berlin 1981, S. 41 – 65.

Salza, R., Der Handwerkslehrling im Dritten Reich, Berlin 1937 (Diss.).

Samuelson, P. A./W. D. Nordhaus, Economics, 17th edition, New York 2001.

Samuelson, P. A./W. D. Nordhaus, Volkswirtschaftslehre, 15. Auflage, Wien/Frankfurt a. M. 1998.

Schädler, K.-F., Der afrikanische Handwerker und die Prozesse seiner beruflichen Qualifikation. In: K. Schaack (Hg.), Grundzüge und Probleme der Entwicklung flächendeckender Berufsbildungssysteme im "frankophonen" Afrika, Mannheim 1983, S. 21 – 33.

Schäffle, A., Bau und Leben des socialen Körpers, Tübingen 1881 (two volumes).

Scheibe, W., Die reformpädagogische Bewegung: 1900 – 1932 – Eine einführende Darstellung, Weinheim und Basel 1999.

Scheler, M., Die Ursachen des Deutschenhasses, Leipzig 1917.

Schimmank, U., In Luhmanns Gesellschaft (Rezension). In: Kölner Zeitschrift für Soziologie und Sozialpsychologie, 50. Jg., Heft 1, März 1998, S. 176 – 181.

Schlaffke, W., Berufsausbildung – eine strategische Aufgabe der Wirtschaft. In: Kuratorium der deutschen Wirtschaft für Berufsbildung (Hg.), Berufsausbildung auf dem Prüfstand – Fachtagung 1993 der gewerblich-technischen Ausbildungsleiter, Bonn 1994, S. 13 – 27.

Schmidt, H., Duales System der Berufsbildung in der Krise? In: A. Ostendorf/H. Sehling (Hrsg.), Berufsbildung im Umbruch, Bielefeld 1996, S. 53 – 58.

Schmuhl, H.-W., Arbeitsmarktpolitik und Arbeitsverwaltung in Deutschland 1871 – 2002, Nürnberg 2003 (Beiträge zur Arbeitsmarkt- und Berufsforschung: BeitrAB 270).

Schoenfeldt, E., Berufsbezug, zentrales Merkmal der deutschen Berufsbildung, Kassel 2002.

Schulz, H., Die Schulreform der Sozialdemokratie, Berlin 1919 (first published 1911).

Schumpeter, J. A., Kapitalismus, Sozialismus und Demokratie, Tübingen und Basel 1993 (7. Auflage).

Schumpeter, J. A., Theorie der wirtschaftlichen Entwicklung – Eine Untersuchung über Unternehmergewinn, Kapital, Kredit, Zins und den Konjunkturzyklus, Berlin 1993 (unveränderter Nachdruck von 1934).

Schwarzfischer, J., Kritik an Kerschensteiner. In: G. Wehle (Hrsg.), Kerschensteiner, Darmstadt 1979, S. 234 – 241 (first published in: Die Deutsche Berufs- und Fachschule, 45 Jg., (1949), S. 432 – 437).

Schwiedrzik, B., Vom Sonderweg für Berufserfahrene ohne Abitur zum "Prinzip Berufserfahrung" – Einleitung. In: K. Mucke/B. Schwiedrzik, Studieren ohne Abitur, Bielefeld 1997.

Seubert, R., Berufserziehung unter dem Nationalsozialismus – Das berufspädagogische Erbe und seine Betreuer, Weinheim – Basel 1977.

Siemsen, A., Beruf und Erziehung, Berlin 1928.

Singleton, J. (ed.), Learning in Likely Places – Varieties of Apprenticeship in Japan, Cambridge – New York 1998.

Sontheimer, K./W. Bleek, Grundzüge des politischen Systems Deutschlands, München 2002 (14. Auflage).

Spaeth, L., Wir bilden falsch aus! In: Handelsblatt, 03. 04. 2003.

Spiewak, M., Penne(n) trotz PISA – Wir brauchen die Gesamtschule, aber ohne die alte Ideologie. In: Die Zeit Nr. 49/2002.

Spranger, E., Berufsbildung und Allgemeinbildung. In: A. Kühne (Hrsg.), Handbuch für das Berufs- und Fachschulwesen, Leipzig 1922, S. 24 – 38.

Spranger, E., Lebensformen – Geisteswissenschaftliche Psychologie und Ethik der Persönlichkeit, Tübingen 1966 (first published in 1914).

Stratmann, Kw., "Zeit der Gärung und Zersetzung" – Arbeiterjugend im Kaiserreich zwischen Schule und Beruf, Weinheim 1992.

Stratmann, Kw., Berufserziehung und sozialer Wandel, Frankfurt am Main 1999.

Stratmann, Kw., Georg Kerschensteiner. Kritische Analyse seiner Pädagogik. In: Kw. Stratmann, Berufsbildung und sozialer Wandel, Frankfurt am Main 1999, S. 631 – 645.

Stratmann, Kw., Zur Sozialgeschichte der Berufsbildungstheorie. In: Zeitschrift für Berufs- und Wirtschaftspädagogik, 84. Band, Oktober 1988, S. 579 – 598.

Stratmann, Kw./M. Schlösser, Das duale System der Berufsbildung – Eine historische Analyse seiner Reformdebatten, Frankfurt/M. 1992.

Streeck, W., Deutscher Kapitalismus: Gibt es ihn? Kann er überleben? In: W. Streeck, Korporatismus in Deutschland – Zwischen Nationalstaat und Europäischer Union, Frankfurt/M. – New York 1999, S. 13 – 40.

Streeck, W., Korporatismus in Deutschland – Zwischen Nationalstaat und Europäischer Union, Frankfurt/M. – New York 1999.

Streeck, W./Ph. C. Schmitter (eds), Private Interest Government – Beyond Market and State, London 1985.

Stütz, G., Berufspädagogik unter ideologiekritischem Aspekt, Frankfurt am Main 1970.

Timmermann, D., Umlagefinanzierung in Eigenregie der Wirtschaft auf Kammerebene. In: Berufsbildung, 51. Jg., Dezember 1997, Nr. 48, S. 24 – 29.

Timmermann, D., Zukunftsprobleme des Dualen Systems unter Bedingungen verschärften Wettbewerbs – Manuskript des Vortrags vom 05. 10. 1989 anlässlich der Jahrestagung des Ausschusses für Bildungsökonomie im Verein für Sozialpolitik in Trier am 05. und 06. Oktober 1989 (mimeo).

Troeltsch, E., Der Geist der deutschen Kultur. In: O. Hintze, F. Meinecke, H. Oncken, H. Schumacher (Hg.), Deutschland und der Weltkrieg, Leipzig und Berlin 1915, S. 52 -90.

Troeltsch, E., Spektator-Briefe: Aufsätze über die deutsche Revolution und die Weltpolitik 1918/1922, Aalen 1966 (reprint of the edition from 1924), S. 52.

Veblen, Th., Imperial Germany and the Industrial Revolution, Ann Arbor 1966, pp. 160 – 162, 170 – 173 (extracts), in: J. B. Mueller (Hg.), Deutschland: Eine westliche Nation – Konzeptionen und Kontroversen, Goldbach 1993, S. 64).

Wander, H., Berufsausbildung und Produktivität, Kiel 1953.

Ware, G. W., Berufserziehung und Lehrlingsausbildung in Deutschland. In: G. Pätzold (Hg.), Die betriebliche Berufsbildung 1945 – 1990, Köln – Wien 1991, S. 231 – 247.

Weber, M., Wirtschaft und Gesellschaft, Tübingen 1980.

Wehle, G. (Hg.), Georg Kerschensteiner, Bd. I: Berufsbildung und Berufsschule – Ausgewählte Pädagogische Schriften, Paderborn 1966.

Wehle, G. (Hg.), Georg Kerschensteiner, Bd. II: Texte zum Pädagogischen Begriff der Arbeit – Ausgewählte Pädagogische Schriften, Paderborn 1982 (2. Auflage).

Wehler, H.-U., The German Empire 1871 – 1918, Oxford – New York 1997 (first English edition: 1985).

Weidenfeld, U., Die große Leere – Das deutsche Ausbildungssystem galt als einzigartig, doch die Zeit hat es überholt. In: Der Tagesspiegel, 17.06. 2004.

Weusthoff, B., Betriebliche Reorganisation und deren Implikationen für die Arbeits- und Lernorganisation am Beispiel der VW Coaching AG. In: P. Dehnbostel/G. Dybowski (Hg.), Lernen, Wissensmanagement und berufliche Bildung, Bielefeld 2000.

Wiemann, G., Didaktische Modelle beruflichen Lernens im Wandel – Vom

Lehrgang zur kunden- und produktionsorientierten Lernorganisation, Bonn 2002.

Wilhelm, Th., Die Pädagogik Kerschensteiners – Vermächtnis und Verhängnis, Stuttgart 1957.

Williams, B., Truth and Truthfulness, Princeton 2002 (Princeton University Press).

Windolf, P., Die Zukunft des Rheinischen Kapitalismus. In: Kölner Zeitschrift für Soziologie und Sozialpsychologie, Sonderheft 42/2002, S. 414 – 442.

Winterhager, W. D., Kosten und Finanzierung der beruflichen Bildung – Eine wirtschaftstheoretische Analyse mit empirischen Daten zur Lehrlingsausbildung in der Industrie, Stuttgart 1969.

Wirth, A. G., Education in the Technological Society – The Vocational-Liberal Studies Controversy in the Early Twentieth Century, Scranton/ Pennsylvania 1972.

Wößmann, L., Letzte Chance für gute Schulen, München 2007.

Wood, St., Business, Government and Patterns of Labour Market Policy in Britain and the Federal Republic of Germany. In: Peter A. Hall/David W. Soskice, Varieties of Capitalism. The Institutional Foundations of Comparative Advantage, Oxford University Press 2001, pp. 247 – 274.